The Complete Book of
Practical Proverbs & Wacky Wit

VERN MCLELLAN

Tyndale House Publishers, Inc.
Wheaton, Illinois

Vern hopes you enjoy the book! If you would like
to contact him, write to:

Vern McLellan
P.O. Box 698
Cathedral City, CA
92235-0698

Unless otherwise stated, Scripture verses are taken from *The Living Bible*, copyright © 1971 owned by
assignment by KNT Charitable Trust. All rights reserved.

Scripture quotations marked KJV are taken from the *Holy Bible*, King James Version.

Scripture quotations marked NIV are taken from the *Holy Bible*, New International Version®. Copyright ©
1973, 1978, 1984 by International Bible Society. Used by permission of Zondervan Publishing House. All
rights reserved. The "NIV" and "New International Version" trademarks are registered in the United States
Patent and Trademark Office by International Bible Society. Use of either trademark requires permission of
International Bible Society.

Library of Congress Cataloging-in-Publication Data

The complete book of practical proverbs and wacky wit / [compiled by] Vernon McLellan.
    p. cm.
    ISBN 0-8423-7851-0 (sc : alk. paper)
    1. Christian life—Quotations, maxims, etc.   2. Bible.   O.T. Proverbs—Devotional use.
I. McLellan, Vernon K.
BV4501.2.C65   1996
242—dc20   95-39479

Printed in the United States of America

02 01 00 99 98 97 96
8   7   6   5   4

Contents

1 Achievement
3 Action
8 Adversity
8 Advice
10 Aim
12 Ambition
14 Arrogance
17 Attitude
19 Authority
21 Booze
23 Bores and Boredom
25 Change
27 Character
30 Christmas
33 Commitment to God
35 Conceit
37 Confidence
39 Conscience
41 Cooperation
43 Correction
45 Courage
47 Creativity
49 Decision Making
51 Diplomacy
53 Direction
55 Discouragement
57 Drinking and Driving

80 Egotism
82 Endurance
84 Experience
88 Failure
71 Faith
74 Father
76 Fear
79 Fools and Foolishness
83 Friendship
87 Fulfillment
89 Future
93 Gambling
95 Giving
97 Gossip
99 Happiness
103 Hearing
105 Help
107 Honesty
109 Hope
111 Horse Sense
113 Humor
116 Ideas
118 Intelligence
120 Joy
122 Judgment
124 Justice
126 Kindness

130 Knowledge
132 Laughter
135 Laziness
137 Leadership
139 Learning
141 Life and Death
143 Love
147 Man/Husband
149 Marriage
153 Mercy
155 Mistakes
157 Money
163 Mother
167 Motivation
169 Mouth/Speech
171 Obedience
173 Opportunity
175 Optimism/Pessimism
179 Parents
183 Persistence
185 Plans
187 Prayer
193 Preparation

195 Pride
197 Problems
200 Promises
202 Quarrels
204 Quietness
206 Reputation
208 Self-Control
210 Success
214 Teaching
216 Temptation
218 Tenacity
221 Thankfulness
223 Time
227 Tomorrow/Today/
    Yesterday
229 Trouble
231 Truth
234 Vision
238 Wisdom
240 Woman/Wife
244 Words
248 Work
250 Zeal

Achievement

If you wait for perfect conditions, you
will never get anything done. . . .
Keep on sowing your seed, for you
never know which will grow—
perhaps it all will.

Ecclesiastes 11:4, 6

Achievement

The father of success is work—the mother of achievement is ambition.

There are four steps to achievement: Plan purposefully. Prepare prayerfully. Proceed positively. Pursue persistently. Failure is the path of least persistence.

After all is said and done, there's more said than done.

Do not mistake activity for achievement.

If God simply handed us everything we wanted, he would be taking from us our greatest prize—the joy of achievement.

There is no limit to what can be accomplished if it doesn't matter who gets the credit. *Ralph Waldo Emerson*

Every day you write your own paycheck.

The three great essentials to achieve anything worthwhile are first, hard work; second, stick-to-itiveness; and third, common sense. *Thomas Edison*

He who wants to make a place in the sun should expect blisters.

Some people dream of worthy achievement, while others stay awake and experience it.

He started to sing as he tackled the thing that couldn't be done, and he did it. *Edgar Guest*

You can tell when you're on the right road—it's uphill.

Action

He wrote [Proverbs] to teach his
people how to live—how to act
in every circumstance.

Proverbs 1:2

———

A man is known by his actions.
An evil man lives an evil life; a
good man lives a godly life.

Proverbs 21:8

———

Don't try to disclaim responsibility
by saying you didn't know about it.
For God, who knows all hearts,
knows yours, and he knows you
knew! And he will reward everyone
according to his deeds.

Proverbs 24:12

Action

It doesn't do a person any good to sit up and take notice if he keeps on sitting.

He who is waiting for something to turn up might start with his own shirtsleeves.

Initiative is doing the right thing at the right time without having to be told.

Between saying and doing, many a pair of shoes is worn out. *Italian proverb*

Men are polished, through *act* and *speech,* each by each as pebbles are smoothed on a rolling beach.

Talk is cheap—*do* something!

I've never heard anything about the resolutions of the apostles, but I have heard a great deal about the acts of the apostles.

I do the best I know how, the very best I can; and I mean to keep on doing it to the end. If the end brings me out all right, what is said against me will not amount to anything. If the end brings me out wrong, ten angels swearing I was right would make no difference. *Abraham Lincoln*

He who starts a journey of a thousand miles begins with one step.

People may doubt what you say, but they'll always believe what you do.

Those who act receive the prizes. *Aristotle*

Do something. Either lead, follow, or get out of the way. *Ted Turner*

The Lord said to Moses, "Quit praying and get the people moving! Forward, march!" *Exodus 14:15*

Action should not be confused with haste. *Lee Iacocca*

Many have the right aim in life, but they never get around to pulling the trigger.

He who is overcautious will accomplish little in life.

The proof of the pudding is in the eating.

What we weave on earth we'll wear in heaven.

Whatsoever thy hand findeth to do, do it with thy might. *Ecclesiastes 9:10, KJV*

Even if you're on the right track, you'll get run over if you just sit there. *Will Rogers*

You cannot make a place for yourself in the sun if you keep sitting in the shade of the family tree.

We cannot help being old, but we can resist being aged.

I am only one, but I am one. I cannot do everything, but I can do something; I will not refuse to do the something that I can do. *Edward Everett Hale*

It's great to have your feet on the ground, but keep them moving.

Adversity

Go ahead and prepare for the conflict,
but victory comes from God.

Proverbs 21:31

———

You are a poor specimen if you can't
stand the pressure of adversity.

Proverbs 24:10

Adversity

A smooth sea never made a skillful mariner.

Adversity tries great men, prosperity the small ones.

Little drops of water wear down big stones. *Russian proverb*

After crosses and losses, men grow humbler and wiser.
Benjamin Franklin

Adversity is the only diet that will reduce a fat head.

Graduation from the university of adversity will help prepare a man for a life of diversity.

Adversity introduces a man to himself.

God brings men into deep waters, not to drown them, but to cleanse them.

When everything seems to be going against you, remember that the airplane takes off *against* the wind, not with it.

If you can't stand the heat, stay out of the kitchen.
Harry Truman

Advice

A fool thinks he needs no advice,
but a wise man listens to others.
Proverbs 12:15

———

Be humble, take advice,
and become wise.
Proverbs 13:10

———

The advice of a wise man refreshes
like water from a mountain spring.
Those accepting it become aware
of the pitfalls on ahead.
Proverbs 13:14

Advice

Advising a fool is like beating the air with a stick.

Advice after injury is like medicine after death.
Danish proverb

Admonish your friends privately, but praise them openly.
Cyrus the Younger, Persian prince

Most people wish to serve God—but only in an advisory capacity.

If you're old, give advice; if you are young, take it.

The football coach challenged his high school team: "Remember, football develops individuality, initiative, and leadership. Now get out there, and do exactly what I tell you."

One thing I've learned in growing old,
No doubt you've noticed too:
The kids to whom you gave advice
Now give advice to you. *F. G. Kernan*

Good advice is no better than poor advice, unless you follow it.

Quite a few people owe their success to advice they didn't take.

Aim

> Have two goals: wisdom—that is, knowing and doing right—and common sense. Don't let them slip away, for they fill you with living energy and bring you honor and respect.
>
> *Proverbs 3:21-22*
>
> ———
>
> Wisdom is the main pursuit of sensible men, but a fool's goals are at the ends of the earth!
>
> *Proverbs 17:24*

A i m

Tend to your goals. He who aims at nothing is sure to hit it.

He who doesn't know where he is going may miss it when he gets there.

There's no point in carrying the ball unless you know where the goal is.

Long-range goals keep you from being frustrated by short-term failures.

It's more important to know where you're going than to see how fast you can get there.

Our plans miscarry because they have no aim. When a man does not know what harbor he is making for, no wind is the right wind.

There's no point in aiming at a target with no arrow in your bow.

Aim high, but stay on the level.

Climb high, climb far; your aim the sky, your goal the star.

Too many people shoot blanks when aiming at their goals.

Aims and ideals are like tuning forks; you must sound them frequently to keep your life up to pitch.

Ambition

Wait for the Lord, and he will come
and save you! Be brave,
stouthearted, and courageous.
Psalm 27:14

Ambition and death are alike in this:
neither is ever satisfied.
Proverbs 27:20

Ambition

A small boy's ambition: to grow up to be a farmer so he can get paid for not raising spinach.

If a man constantly aspires, is he not elevated?
Henry David Thoreau

The first one gets the oyster; the second gets the shell.
Andrew Carnegie

Ambition is a get-ahead-ache.

Too low they build who build beneath the stars.
Edward Young

If at first you don't succeed, try a little ardor.

You do not test the resources of God until you attempt the impossible. *F. B. Meyer*

Behold the turtle. He makes progress only when he sticks his neck out. *James Bryant Conant*

Without a doubt, the easiest undertaking to start from scratch is a flea circus.

All men are created equal, but ambition, or lack of it, soon separates them.

Arrogance

For there are six things the Lord
hates—no, seven: haughtiness, lying,
murdering, plotting evil, eagerness to
do wrong, a false witness, sowing
discord among brothers.

Proverbs 6:16-19

———

Wisdom hates pride, arrogance,
corruption, and deceit of every kind.

Proverbs 8:13

Arrogance

The proud man counts his newspaper clippings—the humble man his blessings. *Bishop Fulton J. Sheen*

Some folks are as proud of their ancestors as if they were responsible for them.

He who looks down on his neighbors is usually living on a bluff.

Many a bee has been drowned in his own honey.

Some folks are so proud and arrogant that they can strut sitting down.

Nature never intended for us to pat ourselves on the back. If she had, our hinges would be different.

He who is carried away by his own importance seldom has far to walk back.

Success that goes to a man's head usually pays a very short visit.

Proud men end in shame, but the meek become wise. *Proverbs 11:2*

A sure cure for arrogance is a visit to the cemetery, where eggheads and boneheads get equal billing.

He who has an inflated opinion of himself is likely a poor judge of human nature.

When you know you've got humility, you've lost it. Humility is to make a right estimate of one's self. *Charles Spurgeon*

Attitude

A relaxed attitude lengthens a man's
life; jealousy rots it away.

Proverbs 14:30

———

Be patient and you will finally win,
for a soft tongue can break
hard bones.

Proverbs 25:15

———

A man who refuses to admit his
mistakes can never be successful. But
if he confesses and forsakes them,
he gets another chance.

Proverbs 28:13

Attitude

Life is a grindstone. But whether it grinds us down or polishes us up depends on us. *L. Thomas Holdcroft*

It's not the outlook, but the uplook that counts.

Don't bother to give God instructions; just report for duty. *Corrie ten Boom*

Give some weeds an inch and they'll take a yard!

Whines are the products of sour grapes.

It isn't hard to make a mountain out of a molehill. Just add a little dirt.

A good thing to remember,
A better thing to do—
Work with the construction gang,
Not with the wrecking crew.

There's no danger of developing eyestrain from getting on the bright side of things.

A famous conductor said, "The most difficult instrument to play is the second fiddle. To find a violinist who can play second fiddle with enthusiasm—that's a problem. But if we have no second fiddles, we have no harmony."

Authority

If a king is kind, honest, and fair,
his kingdom stands secure.

Proverbs 20:28

———

With good men in authority, the
people rejoice; but with the wicked
in power, they groan.

Proverbs 29:2

Authority

Authority makes some people grow, while it makes others swell.

Too many captains run the ship aground. Without a general an army is lost.

Authority is a poor substitute for leadership.

Nothing pleases a little man more than an opportunity to crack a big whip.

If there's anything small, shallow, arrogant, or ugly about a person, giving him a little authority will bring it out.

Authority is like a bank account. The more you draw on it, the less you have.

Nothing intoxicates some people like a sip of authority.

There is just as much authority in the family today as there ever was—only now the children exercise it.

The time to teach obedience to authority is in the playpen instead of the state pen.

Booze

Wine gives false courage; hard liquor
leads to brawls; what fools men are
to let it master them, making them
reel drunkenly down the street!
Proverbs 20:1

O my son, be wise and stay in God's
paths; don't carouse with drunkards
and gluttons, for they are on
their way to poverty.
Proverbs 23:19-20

Booze

Boozers are losers.

There's nothing (or no one) more stubborn than a drunkard trying to convince you he isn't.

Pity the poor boozer who started to get mellow, then he got ripe, and ended up rotten.

Some folks drink liquor as if they want to be mentioned in "BOOZE WHO."

A fool and a drunkard are two of the most mistaken human beings on earth. One thinks he is wise, and the other thinks he is sober.

A boozer insisted that his liquor bill was deductible as a medical expense. "My friends and I drink to each others' health."

Booze makes a man colorful; it gives him a red nose, a white liver, a yellow streak, and a blue outlook.

It's when a man gets as tight as a drum that he makes the most noise.

Booze-befuddled brains bring on brawls, bumps, and bruises.

Drinking is something that makes one lose inhibitions and give exhibitions.

Cars and bars lead to stars and scars.

Bores and Boredom

Don't talk so much. You keep putting
your foot in your mouth. Be sensible
and turn off the flow! When a
good man speaks, he is worth
listening to, but the words of
fools are a dime a dozen.
Proverbs 10:19-20

The backslider gets bored
with himself; the godly man's life
is exciting.
Proverbs 14:14

Bores and Boredom

A bore is someone who tells you his life story from A to Zzzzzzz.

A bore always leaves a person me-deep in conversation.

Boredom is also known as a state of "mine."

Bores are people who bring happiness whenever they go.

The coach was reviewing the highlights of his life and fell asleep.

Some people can stay longer in an hour than others can in a week. *William Dean Howells*

The cure for boredom is curiosity. There is no cure for curiosity. *Ellen Parr*

A bore only stops talking to see if you're still listening.

One good thing about bores is that they don't talk about other people.

There's only one thing worse than a bore, and that's a bore with bad breath.

It's easy to keep from becoming a bore. Just praise the person to whom you're talking.

Change

The good man asks advice from
friends; the wicked plunge
ahead—and fall.
Proverbs 12:26

———

It is pleasant to see plans develop.
That is why fools refuse to give them
up even when they are wrong.
Proverbs 13:19

———

An evil man is stubborn, but a godly
man will reconsider.
Proverbs 21:29

Change

A wise man changes his mind; a fool never does.

It is well for people to change their minds occasionally in order to keep them clean. *Luther Burbank*

Sign on a pastor's desk: "It's too late to agree with me; I've already changed my mind."

The foolish and the dead never change their opinions. *James R. Lowell*

People change, fashions change, and conditions change, but God never changes. *Billy Graham*

There's a small town in Nevada where so little ever changes that the local radio station is still running last year's weather forecasts.

The world changes so fast that you couldn't stay wrong all the time if you tried.

The bamboo that bends is stronger than the oak that resists. *Japanese proverb*

Many people hate any change that doesn't jingle in their pocket.

Character

The character of even a child can be known by the way he acts—whether what he does is pure and right.

Proverbs 20:11

A mirror reflects a man's face, but what he is really like is shown by the kind of friends he chooses.

Proverbs 27:19

The purity of silver and gold can be tested in a crucible, but a man is tested by his reaction to men's praise.

Proverbs 27:21

Character

It's what you do when you have nothing to do that reveals what you are.

Have character—don't be one!

Your character is what you have left when you've lost everything you can lose.

A good character is the best tombstone. Those who loved you, and were helped by you, will remember you when forget-me-nots are withered. Carve your name on hearts, and not on marble. *Charles Spurgeon*

Character is much easier kept than recovered. *Thomas Paine*

How a man plays the game shows something of his character. How he loses shows all of it.

You are what you are when no one is around.

The Lord doesn't take us into deep water to drown us, but to develop us.

Character is what you are in the dark.

A pat on the back develops character—if administered early enough, often enough, and low enough.

The greatest danger facing the United States is not a military lag but a slump in personal and public integrity.
Robert J. McCracken

Life for some people is to sow wild oats during the week and then go to church Sunday and pray for a crop failure.

Ability will enable a man to get to the top, but it takes character to keep him there.

Christmas

Who else holds the wind in his fists
and wraps up the oceans in his cloak?
Who but God has created the world?
If there is any other, what is
his name—and his Son's name—
if you know it?

Proverbs 30:4

For unto us a child is born; unto us a
son is given; and the government
shall be upon his shoulder. These
will be his royal titles: "Wonderful,"
"Counselor," "The Mighty God,"
"The Everlasting Father,"
"The Prince of Peace."

Isaiah 9:6

Christmas

What most mothers want for Christmas is the day after.

Christmas is the time of year when everyone wants his past forgotten and his present remembered.

Anyone who doesn't think that Christmas lasts all year doesn't have a charge card.

Nothing destroys the Christmas spirit faster than looking for a parking place.

Christmas is when we celebrate the birth of the Prince of Peace by giving our kids toy rockets, machine guns, and tanks.

Christmas is the time of the year when Mother has to separate the men from the toys.

A man goes through three stages in his lifetime: First, he believes in Santa; second, he doesn't believe in Santa; and third, he *is* Santa!

Christmas is when Santa comes down the chimney and your savings go down the drain.

Christmas shoppers are the people with the brotherly shove.

One good thing about Christmas shopping—it toughens you up for the January sales.

The shortest night of the year is Christmas Eve from sundown to son-up.

The church bulletin declared, "The choir will sing 'I heard the bills on Christmas Day.'"

Commitment to God

Commit everything you do to
the Lord. Trust him to help you
do it, and he will.

Psalm 37:5

Commit your work to the Lord,
then it will succeed.

Proverbs 16:3

Commitment to God

Guidance means I can count on God. Commitment means God can count on me.

Commitment in the face of conflict produces character.

God does not ask about our ability or our inability, but about our availability.

The world has yet to see what God can do through a man who is fully committed to him.

It doesn't take such a great man to be a Christian; it just takes all there is of him. *Seth Wilson*

Conceit

Sinners love to fight; boasting is
looking for trouble.

Proverbs 17:19

———

When arguing with a rebel, don't use
foolish arguments as he does, or you
will become as foolish as he is! Prick
his conceit with silly replies!

Proverbs 26:4-5

———

There is one thing worse than a fool,
and that is a man who is conceited.

Proverbs 26:12

Conceit

The world's most conceited man is the one who celebrates his birthday by sending flowers and a telegram of congratulations to his mother.

He who is all wrapped up in himself is overdressed.

The self-made man always seems to admire his maker.

The guy who is riding a high horse is heading for a fall.

A big shot is frequently an individual of small caliber and immense bore.

There is something pathetic about a man who turns on his charm when he has none.

Conceit is generally assumed as God's gift to little people.

A conceited person never gets anywhere because he thinks he is already there.

The strength that comes from confidence can quickly be lost in conceit.

The person who believes in nothing but himself lives in a very small world.

The self-made man has relieved his Creator of an embarrassing responsibility.

The fellow who is too deeply in love with himself ought to get a divorce.

Confidence

It is better to trust the Lord than
to put confidence in men. It is better
to take refuge in him than in
the mightiest king!

Psalm 118:8-9

In quietness and in confidence
shall be your strength.

Isaiah 30:15, KJV

Confidence

The line between self-confidence and conceit is very narrow.

Look backward with gratitude and forward with confidence.

The strength that comes from confidence can quickly be lost in conceit.

Confidence is the feeling you have before you fully understand the situation.

A good leader inspires men to have confidence in him; a great leader inspires them to have confidence in themselves.

Confidence is keeping your chin up; overconfidence is sticking your neck out.

Believers eventually become achievers.

He who has lost confidence can lose nothing more. *Boiste*

Mutual confidence is the pillar of friendship.

To whom you give your confidence, to him you resign your liberty.

Conscience

A man's conscience is the Lord's
searchlight exposing his
hidden motives.
Proverbs 20:27

———

The wicked flee when no one is
chasing them! But the godly
are bold as lions!
Proverbs 28:1

Conscience

A conscience is something that hurts us when everything else feels terrific.

The reason most people have a clean conscience is that they never use it.

A good conscience is a continual Christmas.
Benjamin Franklin

There's no pillow so soft as a clear conscience. *French proverb*

Conscience: that still small voice that makes you still smaller.

Most of us follow our conscience as we follow a wheelbarrow. We push it in front of us in the direction we want to go.
Billy Graham

The best tranquilizer is a good conscience.

What the world needs is an amplifier for the still, small voice.

Conscience is something inside that bothers you when nothing outside does.

Cooperation

How wonderful it is, how pleasant,
when brothers live in harmony!
Psalm 133:1

———

Crooks are jealous of each other's
loot, while good men long to
help each other.
Proverbs 12:12

Cooperation

Cooperation is spelled with two letters: we. *G. M. Verity*

Coming together is a beginning; staying together is progress; working together is success.

A steering committee is a group of four people trying to park a car.

No one can whistle a symphony. It takes an orchestra to play it.

You can't applaud with one hand.

If you see a turtle on a stump, you know he didn't get there by himself.

Team spirit: If anything goes bad, I did it. If anything goes real good, then we did it. *Bear Bryant*

Cooperation will solve many problems. Even freckles would be a nice tan if they would get together.

Who passed the ball to you when you scored?

Cooperate! Remember the banana? Every time it leaves the bunch it gets skinned.

We must all hang together, or assuredly we shall all hang separately. *Benjamin Franklin*

Correction

Young man, do not resent it when
God chastens and corrects you, for his
punishment is proof of his love. Just
as a father punishes a son he delights
in to make him better, so the
Lord corrects you.
Proverbs 3:11-12

Anyone willing to be corrected is on
the pathway to life. Anyone refusing
has lost his chance.
Proverbs 10:17

A man who refuses to admit his
mistakes can never be successful. But
if he confesses and forsakes them,
he gets another chance.
Proverbs 28:13

Correction

If you correct yourself, others won't have to.

Spoiled kids soon become little stinkers.

Nothing is harder on a grandparent than having to watch a grandchild being corrected.

The sturdiest tree is not found in the shelter of the forest but high upon some rocky crag, where its daily battle with the elements shapes it into a thing of beauty.

Storms make oaks take deeper roots.

No pain, no palm; no thorns, no throne; no gall, no glory; no cross, no crown. *William Penn*

Crime is not corrected in the electric chair, but in the high chair.

Discipline, once considered "standard household equipment," has fallen on hard times, and in its place permissiveness reigns.

Human beings have willpower, while a mule has won't power.

Courage

A man's courage can sustain his
broken body, but when courage dies,
what hope is left?
Proverbs 18:14

———

The wicked flee when no one is
chasing them! But the godly are
bold as lions!
Proverbs 28:1

Courage

One man with courage makes a majority. *Andrew Jackson*

So what if they're taller? We'll play big! *Coach George Ireland*

No one wants to be brave anymore—just chief!

It's all right to be cautious—but even a turtle never gets anywhere until he sticks his head out.

More twins are being born these days than ever before. Maybe kids lack courage to come into the world alone.

Courage is being the only one who knows you're afraid.

Did you hear about the military inductee who, when asked if he had any defects, replied, "No guts"?

Necessity makes even the timid brave.

Remember, you are your own doctor when it comes to curing cold feet.

People who lack courage think with their legs.

Don't be afraid to go out on a limb. That's where the fruit is.

Keep your fears to yourself, but share your boldness with others.

Creativity

Come, all of you who are skilled
craftsmen having special talents, and
construct what God has commanded
us: . . . So all the people went to their
tents to prepare their gifts.

Exodus 35:10,20

———

Do not despise this small beginning,
for the eyes of the Lord rejoice to
see the work begin.

Zechariah 4:10

Creativity

The reason ideas die quickly in some people's heads is that they can't stand solitary confinement.

God gives the nuts, but he does not crack them.

A new idea is delicate. It can be killed by a sneer or a yawn, stabbed to death by a quip, or worried to death by a frown.

Another war worth waging is one against the poverty of ideas.

The mind once stretched by a great idea can never return to its original dimensions.

Happiness lies in the joy of achievement and the thrill of creative effort. *Franklin D. Roosevelt*

The best way to put an idea across is to wrap it in a person.

Getting a new idea should be like sitting on a tack; it should make you get up and do something about it.

Louis Pasteur had nothing to work with but the germ of an idea.

When man learned that he could not live by bread alone, he invented the sandwich. *Bob Barnes*

The fellow who invented the eraser had the human race pretty well sized up.

Decision Making

We should make plans—counting
on God to direct us.
Proverbs 16:9

We toss the coin, but it is the Lord
who controls its decision.
Proverbs 16:33

What a shame—yes, how stupid!—to
decide before knowing the facts!
Proverbs 18:13

Decision Making

The reason most people change their minds is that they never find one worth keeping.

One of these days is none of these days. *English proverb*

Before you start looking for a peg, decide which hole you want to fill.

Never make a decision based on fear.

Making decisions is simple: Get the facts; seek God's guidance; form a judgment; act on it; worry no more.
Charles E. Bennett

An executive is a guy who can take as long as he wants to make a snap decision.

A wise man makes his own decisions; an ignorant man follows public opinion. *Chinese proverb*

One of the hardest decisions to make in life is when to start middle age.

Almost everyone knows the difference between right and wrong, but some just hate to make decisions. *Joseph Salak*

The answer is maybe—and that's final!

Diplomacy

A man is a fool to trust himself! But
those who use God's wisdom are safe.

Proverbs 28:26

Diplomacy

Diplomacy is a peaceful substitute for shooting.

Diplomacy is the ability to take something and make the other fellow believe he is giving it away.

A diplomat possesses the art of handling a porcupine without disturbing the quills.

Diplomacy is the ability to give the other guy a shot in the arm without letting him feel the needle.

Arch Ward says that tact is the ability to shut your mouth before someone else wants to.

The person who is tactful has the knack of making a point without making an enemy.

The hostess who is tactful has the ability to make guests feel at home when that's where she wishes they were.

Tact is powdering your own no's.

Tact is rubbing out another's mistake instead of rubbing it in.

A tactless person says what everyone else is thinking.

A diplomat can bring home the bacon without spilling the beans.

Direction

In everything you do, put God first,
and he will direct you and crown your
efforts with success.

Proverbs 3:6

———

Since the Lord is directing our steps,
why try to understand everything that
happens along the way?

Proverbs 20:24

Direction

Did you hear about the cross-eyed discus thrower? He didn't set any records—but he sure kept the crowd awake.

If at first you don't succeed, try reading the directions.

A stranger in town asked a shoe-shine boy if he could direct him to the bank. "I will for a quarter," replied the boy. "Isn't that pretty high?" asked the man. "Not for a bank director," replied the lad.

You can tell when you are on the right road—it's all uphill.

This fast age seems more concerned about speed than direction.

If you don't know where you're going, any road will get you there.

Where you go hereafter depends on *what* you go after here.

When people start off on the right foot, there's a better chance that they'll get in step sooner.

No wind is favorable for the sailor who doesn't know which direction he is going.

If you don't know where you're going, you will wind up somewhere else. *Yogi Berra*

Wherever you go, there you are.

There are no shortcuts to any place worth going.

Discouragement

Gentle words cause life and health;
griping brings discouragement.

Proverbs 15:4

Anxious hearts are very heavy, but a
word of encouragement does wonders!

Proverbs 12:25

Hope deferred makes the heart sick;
but when dreams come true at last,
there is life and joy.

Proverbs 13:12

Discouragement

Never let discouragement be carried over into a new day.

If the enemy can't puff you up with pride, he will try to dampen your spirit by discouragement. It's his best tool!

Discouragement is faith in the devil.

Most men fail, not through lack of education, but from lack of dogged determination and dauntless will. *Charles Swindoll*

It's not the size of the dog in the fight, but the size of the fight in the dog that makes the difference.

When down in the mouth remember Jonah—he came out all right. *Thomas Edison*

And let us not get tired of doing what is right, for after a while we will reap a harvest of blessing if we don't get discouraged and give up. *Galatians 6:9*

Disappointment should always be taken as a stimulant, and never viewed as a discouragement.

The person who has not struggled with difficulty and discouragement cannot know the joy of genuine success. Face your problems and fight your way through them. There is more satisfaction in putting forth effort than gloating over easily won profits. The rungs on the ladder of success are composed of difficulties.

The world at its worst demands Christians at their best—on top of the circumstances.

Drinking and Driving

The man who strays away from
common sense will end up dead!
Proverbs 21:16

Drinking and Driving

Traffic warning sign: "Heads you win—cocktails you lose."

He who has one for the road gets a trooper for a chaser.

Watch out for schoolchildren—especially those who are driving.

Drive to arrive alive.

It would be better to be a little late down here than too early up there.

The life of the party may also become the death of the highway.

Stop and think before you drink.

Drive sensibly and responsibly. If you don't, your present car may last you a lifetime.

A Sunday school teacher was describing how Lot's wife looked back and suddenly turned into a pillar of salt. "My mother looked back once while she was driving," contributed little Johnny, "and she turned into a telephone pole."

Seat belts are not as confining as wheelchairs.

The driver who weaves through traffic may wind up getting stitched.

If you think I'm a bad driver, you ought to see me putt.
Bumper sticker

Always try to drive so that your license will expire before you do.

Egotism

Don't praise yourself; let others do it!

Proverbs 27:2

Egotism

The egotist says, "Everyone has a right to my opinion."

People on ego trips should do others a favor and buy one-way tickets.

An egomaniac is someone who's hard of listening.

Blowing one's horn only succeeds in deafening the listener.

The fact is, egomania is a form of I-dolatry.

People who are all wrapped up in themselves usually make pretty small packages.

An egomaniac is a self-made man who insists on giving everyone the recipe.

An egomaniac enters the room, dragging his tale behind him.

A self-centered fellow is a guy who deprives you of privacy without providing any company.

An egomaniac not only holds a conversation but strangles it.

There's this to be said for egomaniacs: The more you think of them, the less you think of them.

People who sing their own praises often find themselves singing a solo.

Endurance

They that wait upon the Lord shall
renew their strength. They shall
mount up with wings like eagles; they
shall run and not be weary; they shall
walk and not faint.

Isaiah 40:31

Endurance

Endurance test: entertaining a pest who says nothing, or listening to a bore who does all the talking.

Fortitude: the courage with which some people go through life bearing the misfortunes of others.

Enjoy what you can; endure what you must. *Goethe*

Thank God for the iron in the blood of our fathers. *Theodore Roosevelt*

God will lead you to no waters he cannot part, no brink he cannot cross, no pain he cannot bear.

Today's mighty oak is just yesterday's nut that held its ground.

He who cannot endure tough times will not see good times.

'Tis a lesson you should heed,
Try, try again.
If at first you don't succeed,
Try, try again. *William E. Hickson*

When you get into a tight place and everything goes against you till it seems as though you could not hold on a minute longer, never give up then, for that is just the place and time that the tide will turn. *Harriet Beecher Stowe*

Don't pray for an easier life; pray to be a stronger person.

Experience

I have been young and now I am old.
And in all my years I have never seen
the Lord forsake a man who loves
him; nor have I seen the children of
the godly go hungry.
Psalm 37:25

———

The glory of young men is their
strength; of old men, their experience.
Proverbs 20:29

Experience

Experience should be a guidepost and not a hitching post.

Read the history books and see—for we were born but yesterday and know so little; our days here on earth are as transient as shadows. But the wisdom of the past will teach you. The experience of others will speak to you. *Job 8:8-10*

The taste of defeat has a richness of experience all its own. *Bill Bradley*

Experience is what you have left when everything else is gone.

Experience is about the cheapest thing a fellow can get if he's smart enough to get it secondhand.

Good judgment comes from experience. Experience comes from bad judgment. *Mark Twain*

Burned children spurn the fire.

A wise man learns by the experiences of others. An ordinary man learns by his own experience. A fool learns by nobody's experience.

Experience may be the best teacher, but the one I had in grammar school was much prettier. *Don McNeill*

No matter how hard you try to improve on Mother Nature, you're not kidding Father Time. What Mother Nature giveth, Father Time taketh away.

He who stumbles twice over the same stone deserves to break his shins.

Experience is a form of knowledge acquired only two ways—by doing and being done.

The best substitute for experience is being sixteen.

Experience is what you get when you were expecting something else.

Experience is the worst teacher; it gives the test before explaining the lesson. *Laurence Peter*

Experience is the name everyone gives to his mistakes.

Sixty-five is the age at which one acquires sufficient experience to lose his job.

Very few people listen to the voice of experience—they heed only a kick in the pants.

Once bitten, twice shy.

There are no vacations from the school of experience.

There is only one thing more painful than learning from experience, and that is *not* learning from experience.

Personnel directors of large corporations are looking for men between twenty-five and thirty-five with forty years of experience.

Education is what you get from reading the small print in a contract. Experience is what you get from *not* reading it.

Experience is yesterday's answer to today's problems.

Experience is compulsory education.

Those who cannot remember the past are condemned to repeat it.

One thing about the school of experience is that it will repeat the lesson if you flunk the first time.

If you could sell your experience for what it cost, you would never need Social Security. *Ben Bergor*

Experience makes a person bitter or better.

Experience is not only an expensive teacher, but by the time you get through her school, life is over.

Some people profit by their experiences; others never recover from them.

Experience is what you've got when you're too old to get a job.

We learn from experience. A man never wakes up his second baby just to see it smile.

One reason experience is such a good teacher is that she doesn't allow any dropouts.

There's no free tuition in the school of experience.

Every time you graduate from the school of experience someone thinks up a graduate program.

Unused experience is a dead loss.

Experience is one thing you can't get on the easy installment plan.

A person becomes wise by observing what happens when he isn't.

Our wisdom usually comes from our experience, and our experience comes largely from our foolishness.

Failure

> The wise man is glad to be instructed,
> but a self-sufficient fool falls flat
> on his face.
> *Proverbs 10:8*
>
> ———
>
> Pride goes before destruction and
> haughtiness before a fall.
> *Proverbs 16:18*

Failure

The only thing in life achieved without effort is failure.

The gap between enthusiasm and indifference is filled with failures.

The train of failure usually runs on the track of laziness.

Failure is a better teacher than success, but she seldom finds an apple on her desk.

There are a great many more trapdoors to failure than there are to success.

Success comes in cans; failure comes in can'ts.

Failure isn't bitter if you don't swallow it.

Falling down doesn't make you a failure, but staying down does.

God gave each of us two ends—one to sit on and one to think with. A person's success or failure depends on the one he uses most.

Failure is not necessarily missing the target, but aiming too low.

Stopping at third base to congratulate yourself adds no more to the score than striking out.

Failure is the path of least persistence.

Don't hug your failures. Analyze your successes.

In war, there is no substitute for victory. *Douglas MacArthur*

Faith

Trust in your money and down
you go! Trust in God and flourish
as a tree!

Proverbs 11:28

———

God blesses those who obey him;
happy the man who puts his trust
in the Lord.

Proverbs 16:20

Faith

If doubt overtakes you, stop for a faith lift.

Faith is not a pill you take but a muscle you use.

Faith says, "I will give it before I get it."

Christian faith helps us to face the music, even when we don't like the tune.

Feed your faith, and your doubts will starve to death.

He who prays for rain should always carry an umbrella.

Pray for faith that will not shrink when it is washed in the waters of affliction.

There are a thousand ways of pleasing God, but not one without faith.

When we do what we can, God will do what we can't.

Some people ask the Lord to guide them; then they grab the steering wheel.

Faith hears the inaudible, sees the invisible, believes the incredible, and receives the impossible.

Faith can rewrite your future.

It is impossible for faith to overdraw its account on the bank of heaven.

Faith is telling a mountain to move and being shocked only if it doesn't.

Father

Young man, obey your father and your
mother. Take to heart all of their
advice; keep in mind everything
they tell you.

Proverbs 6:20-21

It is a wonderful heritage to have
an honest father.

Proverbs 20:7

A wise son makes his father happy,
but a lad who hangs around with
prostitutes disgraces him.

Proverbs 29:3

Father

Advice to fathers over fifty: Keep an open mind and a closed refrigerator.

By the time a man finds greener pastures, he's too old to climb the fence.

To really know a father, observe his behavior with a lady, a flat tire, and a child.

Judging by church attendance, heaven will not be crowded with men.

Listen, men: Maybe you'll never be as big a hero as your son thinks you are, but you'll never be as big a fool as your mother-in-law thinks you are either!

Some fathers remind us of blisters; they don't show up until after the work is done.

It's hard to raise a family—especially in the morning.

A happy family is like a baseball team—with Mom pitching, Dad catching, the kids fielding, and everyone taking a turn at bat.

Fear

But all who listen to [Wisdom] shall
live in peace and safety, unafraid.

Proverbs 1:33

———

With [wisdom and common sense] on
guard you can sleep without fear; you
need not be afraid of disaster or the
plots of wicked men, for the Lord is
with you; he protects you.

Proverbs 3:24-26

Fear

Courage is fear that has said its prayers.

If a man carries his own lantern, he need not fear darkness.

Don't be afraid to take a big step if it's required. You can't cross a chasm in two small jumps.

Don't fear tomorrow; God is already there.

Fear is the darkroom where the devil takes you to develop your negatives.

Fear and faith cannot keep house together; when one enters, the other departs.

Fear is simply unbelief parading in disguise.

Feed your faith, and your fears will starve to death.

Fear knocked at the door. Faith answered. No one was there.

"How do you know you were going only fifteen miles an hour?" the judge asked the driver accused of speeding. He replied, "I was on my way to the dentist!"

An atheist approaching the end of his life voiced one regret: "There is one thing that mars the pleasures of my life—if I could know that death is an eternal sleep, I would die happy; but this fear pierces my soul—if the Bible is true then I am lost forever."

Fear usually comes as the result of ignorance.

Keep your fears to yourself, but share your courage with others. *Robert Louis Stevenson*

Fools and Foolishness

A wise man thinks ahead; a fool
doesn't and even brags about it!
Proverbs 13:16

———

The wise man looks ahead. The fool
attempts to fool himself and
won't face facts.
Proverbs 14:8

———

A man may ruin his chances by his
own foolishness and then blame it
on the Lord!
Proverbs 19:3

Fools & Foolishness

Think before you speak; silent sense is better than fluent folly.

Observation: You're making a fool of yourself, and I've never seen better craftsmanship.

Life is just one fool thing after another. Love is just two fool things after each other.

Never let a fool kiss you—and never let a kiss fool you.

He is no fool who gives up what he cannot keep to gain what he cannot lose. *Jim Elliot*

It is never wise to argue with a fool; the bystander does not know which is which.

A fool does in the end what the wise man does at the beginning.

The fool wanders; the wise man travels.

Wise men think without talking; fools talk without thinking.

Fools grow without watering.

The fool who doesn't speak sounds like a sage.

The fool declares: "I never make misteaks!"

A wise man's words are few, but a fool only opens his mouth to change feet.

A fool and his money are soon partying.

Even a fish wouldn't get into trouble if it kept its mouth shut.

Fools run in where fools have been before.

The best way to convince a fool that he is wrong is to let him have his own way. *Josh Billings*

If 50 million people say a foolish thing, it is still a foolish thing. *Anatole France*

Fool me once—shame on you! Fool me twice—shame on me!

Only a fool argues with a skunk, a mule, or a cook.

Only fools test the depth of the water with both feet.

The fool uses his reserve—and does not replace it.

Stupidity is forever; ignorance can be fixed.

To try to undo what has been done or agonize over lost opportunities is not only foolish but futile.

Advice is that which the wise don't need and the fools won't take.

Every person has the right to make a fool of himself if he wants to, but it seems too many folks are abusing the privilege.

Adverse criticism from a wise man is more desirable than the enthusiastic approval of a fool.

A fool and his money are soon parted. The rest of us wait until we reach the supermarket.

You've never heard of a woman making a fool out of a man without a lot of cooperation.

Preachers and lawyers are paid for zeal, but fools dish it out for nothing.

Wise people sometimes change their minds—fools, never!

There are two kinds of fools: those who can't change their opinions and those who won't.

Friendship

A true friend is always loyal, and
a brother is born to help in
time of need.
Proverbs 17:17

Faithful are the wounds of a friend;
but the kisses of an enemy
are deceitful.
Proverbs 27:6, KJV

A friendly discussion is as
stimulating as the sparks that fly
when iron strikes iron.
Proverbs 27:17

Friendship

He who walks in when others walk out is a true friend.

The best way to wipe out a friendship is to sponge on it.

Friends are God's life preservers.

You cannot shake hands with a clenched fist. *Golda Meir*

Speak well of your enemies—you made them.

Real friends are those who, when you've made a fool of yourself, don't feel that you've done a permanent job.

Be slow in choosing a friend, slower to change.
Benjamin Franklin

Before borrowing money from a friend, decide which you need most. *American proverb*

If you want an accounting of your worth, count your friends.
Merry Browne

Real friends don't care if your socks don't match.

Nothing in the world is friendlier than a wet dog.

Chance makes our parents, but choice makes our friends.

A friend is a person who knows all about you and still loves you just the same.

Friends are people who stick together 'til debt do them part.

The world needs more warm hearts and fewer hot heads.

Am I not destroying my enemies when I make friends of them? *Abraham Lincoln*

A friend is a person who goes around saying nice things about you behind your back.

Perhaps you've heard the story about the two janitors in a large office building who became fine friends. They were broom mates; they even swept together; in fact, they were dust inseparable.

The reason a dog is a man's best friend is because he does not pretend; he proves it.

The best vitamin for developing friends is B_1.

He who has a thousand friends
Has not a friend to spare,
And he who has one enemy
Will meet him everywhere.

Friendships flourish at the fountain of forgiveness.
William Arthur Ward

The best mirror is an old friend.

Those who seek faultless friends remain friendless.

You're such a good friend; have you ever thought of turning pro?

Always keep your head up—but be careful to keep your nose at a friendly level.

To brighten a friend's life is to increase the wattage of your own.

On the road between the homes of friends, grass does not grow. *Norwegian proverb*

Toast: May the roof over us never fall in, and may we friends gathered below never fall out.

The best way to test a man's friendship is to ask him to co-sign on your note. If he refuses, he is your friend.

Question: If you were somebody else, would you want to be friends with you?

The more arguments you win, the fewer friends you'll own.

Enemies will see through you; friends will see you through.

It's smart to pick your friends—but not to pieces.

Fulfillment

Ill-gotten gain brings no lasting
happiness; right living does.

Proverbs 10:2

———

Telling the truth gives a man great
satisfaction, and hard work returns
many blessings to him.

Proverbs 12:14

———

Hope deferred makes the heart sick;
but when dreams come true at last,
there is life and joy.

Proverbs 13:12

Fulfillment

He who chooses a job he likes will never have to work a day in his life.

If you don't get everything you want, think of the things you don't get that you don't want.

He is well paid that is well satisfied. *William Shakespeare*

In the world there are only two tragedies. One is not getting what one wants and the other is getting it.

Life's greatest fulfillments include getting the last laugh, having the last word, and paying the last installment.

There's no thrill in easy sailing,
When the sky is clear and blue.
There's no joy in merely doing
Things which anyone can do.
But there is some fulfillment
That is mighty sweet to take,
When you reach a destination,
You thought you couldn't make.

Here are five keys to fulfillment: Obey the great God; dream great dreams; plan great plans; pray great prayers; claim great victories.

Even if you're on the right track, you'll get run over if you just sit there. *Will Rogers*

Almost anything can be bought at a reduced price except lasting satisfaction.

Future

The wise man saves for the future,
but the foolish man spends
whatever he gets.
Proverbs 21:20

———

Don't envy evil men but continue
to reverence the Lord all the time,
for surely you have a wonderful
future ahead of you. There is
hope for you yet!
Proverbs 23:17-18

———

Don't envy the wicked. Don't covet
his riches. For the evil man has no
future; his light will be snuffed out.
Proverbs 24:19-20

Future

Where you go hereafter depends on what you go after here.

My interest is in the future because I'm going to spend the rest of my life there.

January 1: "I resolve to be optimistic about the future—if there is one!"

Hats off to the past; sleeves up for the future.

He gave her a smile with a future in it.

Never be afraid to trust an unknown future to an all-knowing God. *Corrie ten Boom*

The future belongs to those who prepare for it.

Never put off until tomorrow what you can do today. If you wait until tomorrow, they will have probably passed a law prohibiting it.

Tomorrow is the day that's always on its way, yet never arrives—unless you have a payment due!

One thing the future *can* guarantee—anything can happen.

Notice on a college bulletin board: "Owing to unfortunate circumstances, our course—Predicting Your Future—has had to be canceled."

The worst thing about the future is that it seems to get here quicker than it used to.

It's better to look where you're going than to see where you've been.

Telling children that school days are the happiest days of their lives doesn't give them much to anticipate.

A vital faith gives us the courage to face the present with confidence and the future with expectancy.

Those who fear the future are likely to fumble the present.

Fear of the future is a waste of the present.

Judging from the way things look, it's a good thing the future doesn't come all at once.

No matter how much a person dreads the future, he usually wants to be around to see it.

Most of us spend a lot of time dreaming of the future, never realizing that a little of it arrives each day.

We make our future by the best use of the present.

Some carve out the future while others just whittle away the time.

It's a great idea to take an interest in the future—that's where you'll spend the rest of your life.

The trouble with the future is that it usually arrives before we're ready for it.

If you've mortgaged the future to buy present pleasure, don't complain when the foreclosure comes.

The time to get primed for the future is when you're still in your prime.

The future frightens only those who prefer living in the past.

We may not know what the future holds, but we know *who* holds the future.

Many fortune-tellers are quitting the business. They claim the future isn't what it used to be.

The future is as bright as the promises of God.

The trouble with growing old is that there's not much future in it.

A pessimist burns his bridges before he gets to them.

A pessimist can hardly wait for the future so he can look back with regret.

There are better things ahead than any we leave behind.
C. S. Lewis

Gambling

The good man is covered with
blessings from head to foot, but an
evil man inwardly curses his luck.

Proverbs 10:6

———

Wealth from gambling quickly
disappears; wealth from
hard work grows.

Proverbs 13:11

Gambling

A visitor to Las Vegas was so unlucky he lost his shirt in a coin laundry.

A race horse is an animal that can take several thousand people for a ride at the same time.

Gambling is just plain stealing by mutual consent.

People who can afford to gamble don't need money, and those who need money can't afford to gamble.

Choice, not chance, determines destiny.

A rabbit's foot is a poor substitute for horse sense.

Good luck often has the odor of perspiration on it.

Luck is what happens when preparation meets opportunity.

Industry is the mother of success—luck, a distant relative.

The best way to get out of a poker game with a small fortune is to start with a large one.

Never gamble in heavy traffic. The cars may be stacked against you.

No horse can go as fast as the money you bet on him.

Gambling is like diving into an empty swimming pool. The chances that you'll hit bottom are about the same.

Giving

Honor the Lord by giving him the first part of all your income, and he will fill your barns with wheat and barley and overflow your wine vats with the finest wines.

Proverbs 3:9-10

It is possible to give away and become richer! It is also possible to hold on too tightly and lose everything. Yes, the liberal man shall be rich! By watering others, he waters himself.

Proverbs 11:24-25

Giving

First, give yourself to God. You may be sure he'll look after what is his.

He gives twice who gives quickly. *Italian proverb*

The hardest thing to give is in.

You have never really lived until you've done something for somebody who can never repay you.

Blessed are those who can give without remembering and take without forgetting.

He who gives when he is asked has waited too long.

The millionaires in eternity are the givers in time.

The best thing you can give someone is a chance.

When it comes to giving, some people stop at nothing.

If you are not generous with a meager income, you will never be generous with abundance. *Harold Nye*

You only keep what you give away. *R. E. Phillips*

Do your giving while you're living, so you're knowing where it's going.

We make a living by what we get, but we make a life by what we give.

Gossip

A gossip goes around spreading
rumors, while a trustworthy man
tries to quiet them.
Proverbs 11:13

———

Don't tell your secrets to a gossip
unless you want them broadcast
to the world.
Proverbs 20:19

———

Fire goes out for lack of fuel, and
tensions disappear when gossip stops.
Proverbs 26:20

Gossip

Gossip is something that goes in one ear and in another.

Conversation is an exercise of the mind, but gossiping is merely an exercise of the tongue.

The paradox about gossips is that they always talk about things that left them speechless.

A gossip is someone who snares the unsuspecting in a mouth trap.

A gossip can give you all the details without knowing any of the facts.

The quickest way to stop gossip is for everyone to shut up.

Gossip is nothing more than mouth-to-mouth recitation.

A gossip compensates for a limited vocabulary with a large turnover.

Gossips burn so much oxygen at the mouth that there's never any left for the brain.

A gossiper is a newscaster without a sponsor.

In most beauty parlors the gossip alone would curl your hair.

Happiness

Wisdom is a tree of life to those who
eat her fruit; happy is the man who
keeps on eating it.

Proverbs 3:18

He that is of a merry heart hath
a continual feast.

Proverbs 15:15, KJV

Pleasant sights and good reports
give happiness and health.

Proverbs 15:30

Happiness

Most people are about as happy as they make up their minds to be. *Abraham Lincoln*

Grudges are clots in the arteries leading to a happy heart. *Frank Tyger*

Happiness is a rebound from hard work.

Happiness walks on busy feet.

The really happy man is the one who can enjoy the scenery even when he has to take a detour.

Happiness is a direction, not a destination.

Happiness is a way station between too much and too little.

Happiness is not the absence of conflict, but the ability to cope with it.

The roots of happiness grow deepest in the soil of service.

The secret of happy living is not to do what you like but to like what you do.

Happiness is something that comes into our lives through a door we don't remember leaving open.

The grand essentials for happiness are something to do, something to love, something to hope for. *John Chalmers*

Happiness is discovering that the slip of paper under your windshield is just an advertisement.

The road to happiness is always under construction.

The thing that counts the most in the pursuit of happiness is choosing the right traveling companion.

Happiness is having a scratch for every itch. *Ogden Nash*

A small house will hold as much happiness as a big one.

For every minute you are angry, you lose sixty seconds of happiness.

Genuine happiness occurs when a wife sees a double chin on her husband's old girlfriend.

The heart is happiest when it beats for others.

Happiness is like a potato salad—when shared with others, it's a picnic.

The secret of happiness is to count your blessings while others are adding up their troubles.

Happiness is like jam—you can't spread even a little without getting some on yourself.

Happiness consists of activity. It's a running stream, not a stagnant pool.

Happiness increases the more you spread it around.

Happiness is being too sick to go to school, but not too sick to watch television.

Some people bring happiness to others wherever they go—others, when.

Happiness is the feeling you're feeling when you want to keep on feeling it.

It isn't our position but our disposition that makes us happy.

Happiness consists of living each day as if it were the first day of your honeymoon and the last day of your vacation.

Happiness is learning that your daughter's boyfriend has had his electric guitar repossessed by the finance company.

When happiness gets into your system, it is bound to break out on your face.

Happiness is not perfected until it is shared.

Happiness is pursuing something but not catching it—unless it's a bus on a rainy night.

Hearing

Wisdom shouts in the streets for a hearing. She calls out to the crowds along Main Street, and to the judges in their courts, and to everyone in all the land.

Proverbs 1:20-21

A fool thinks he needs no advice, but a wise man listens to others.

Proverbs 12:15

Hearing

We have two ears and only one tongue in order that we may hear more and speak less. *Diogenes*

A wise old owl lived in an oak;
The more he saw, the less he spoke;
The less he spoke, the more he heard;
Why can't we all be like that bird?

It's easy to entertain some people. All you have to do is sit and listen.

No man ever listened himself out of a job. *Calvin Coolidge*

Once a man learns how to listen, he and his wife can remain on speaking terms indefinitely.

The first step to wisdom is silence; the second is listening.

The one who listens is the one who understands.

A winner listens; a loser can't wait until it's his turn to talk.

There are two kinds of bores—those who talk too much and those who listen too little.

You can win more friends with your ears than with your mouth.

Help

Don't refuse to accept criticism; get
all the help you can.

Proverbs 23:12

———

Never abandon a friend—either yours
or your father's. Then you won't need
to go to a distant relative for help
in your time of need.

Proverbs 27:10

Help

The best place to find a helping hand is at the end of your own arm.

It's nice to know that when you help someone up a hill you're a little closer to the top yourself.

True charity is helping those you have every reason to believe would not help you.

Criticism should always leave a person with the feeling he has been helped.

Many a man who is too tired to help around the house plays golf for exercise.

It's better to keep a friend from falling than to help him up after he falls.

Offering good advice may be noble and grand, but it's not the same as a helping hand.

To feel sorry for the needy is not the mark of a Christian—to help them is.

It is easier to point a finger than to offer a helping hand.

The open hand holds more friends than the closed fist.

A good way to forget your troubles is to help others out of theirs.

Honesty

The Lord hates cheating and
delights in honesty.

Proverbs 11:1

———

Good people are directed by their
honesty; the wicked shall fall
beneath their load of sins.

Proverbs 11:5

———

Lies will get any man into trouble,
but honesty is its own defense.

Proverbs 12:13

Honesty

Regardless of policy, honesty is easier on the nerves.

The whole art of government consists in the art of being honest. *Thomas Jefferson*

The badge of honesty is simplicity.

It matters not what you do—
Make a nation or a shoe;
For he who does an honest thing
In God's pure sight is ranked a king. *John Parnell*

Even a little lie is dangerous; it deteriorates the conscience. And the importance of conscience is eternal, like love.
Pablo Casals

Not keeping an appointment is an act of clear dishonesty. You may as well borrow a person's money as his time.

It takes an honest person to admit if he's tired or just lazy.

He who loses honesty has nothing else to lose.

There's one way to find out if a man is honest—ask him. If he says yes, you know he is a crook. *Groucho Marx*

An honest man is the noblest work of God. *Alexander Pope*

Hope

The hope of good men is eternal
happiness; the hopes of evil men
are all in vain.

Proverbs 10:28

———

When an evil man dies, his hopes all
perish, for they are based upon
this earthly life.

Proverbs 11:7

———

When you enjoy becoming wise, there
is hope for you! A bright future
lies ahead.

Proverbs 24:14

Hope

The best bridge between hope and despair is often a good night's sleep.

Never live in hope and expectation with your arms folded.

Probably nothing in the world arouses more false hopes than the first four hours of a diet.

As we journey through life, the thing we long for is hope. There is no greater source of hope than God's Word. *Sandi Patty*

Lost hope is the undertaker's best friend.

We are never beneath hope while above hell; nor are we above hope while beneath heaven.

He who lives in hope dances without a fiddle.

Hope is grief's best music.

Life without hope is a life without meaning.

When you say a situation or a person is hopeless, you are slamming the door in the face of God. *Charles L. Allen*

A man hopes that his lean years are behind him; a woman, that hers are ahead.

Hope is putting faith to work when doubting would be easier.

Horse Sense

Everyone admires a man with good sense, but a man with a warped mind is despised.

Proverbs 12:8

———

A man with good sense is appreciated. A treacherous man must walk a rocky road.

Proverbs 13:15

———

My son, how I will rejoice if you become a man of common sense. Yes, my heart will thrill to your thoughtful, wise words.

Proverbs 23:15-16

Horse Sense

Horse sense (another breed of common sense) vanishes when you begin to feel your oats.

It takes a lot of horse sense to maintain a stable life.

Automobiles wouldn't be so dangerous if the horsepower of the engine were proportioned to the horse sense of the driver.

Horse sense is stable thinking coupled with the ability to say nay.

A rabbit's foot is a poor substitute for horse sense.

Horse sense is what keeps horses from betting on what people will do.

There is just as much horse sense as ever, but it seems the horses have it.

It is generally agreed that some people are wise and some are otherwise.

Common sense isn't as common as it used to be. *Will Rogers*

Man was given five senses: touch, taste, sight, smell, and hearing. The successful man has two more: horse and common.

Humor

A cheerful heart does good like
medicine, but a broken spirit
makes one sick.
Proverbs 17:22

———

There is a right time for
everything: . . . a time to laugh. . . .
Ecclesiastes 3:1, 4

Humor

If you don't have a sense of humor, you probably don't have any sense at all.

Humor isn't just a joke now and then; it is a basic survival tool.

The best sense of humor belongs to the fellow who can laugh at himself.

Humor is the hole that lets the sawdust out of a stuffed shirt.

Get-well cards have become so humorous that if you don't get sick you're missing a lot of fun.

I would wish less to go to heaven if I knew that God would not understand a joke. *Martin Luther*

Humor is a lifeboat we use on life's river.

A sense of humor is the pole that adds balance to our steps as we walk the tightrope of life. *William Arthur Ward*

When you think of having a woman for president, that's no problem. What's worrisome is the thought of having a man for first lady!

Wit is the spice of conversation.

Brevity is the soul of wit. *William Shakespeare*

Next to being witty yourself, the best thing is to quote another's wit.

I never lack material for my humor column when Congress is in session. *Will Rogers*

A sense of humor reduces people and problems to their proper proportions.

Humor is the lubricating oil of business. It prevents friction and wins goodwill.

After God created the world, he made man and woman. Then, to keep the whole thing from collapsing, he invented humor. *Guillermo Mordillo*

Ideas

Do not despise this small beginning,
for the eyes of the Lord rejoice to see
the work begin.
Zechariah 4:10

Ideas

Don't just entertain new ideas—put them to work.

The trouble with a public address system is that it amplifies a speaker's voice, but not his ideas. *Martin J. Beckman*

The fellow who invented the Life Saver really made a mint. *Gordon Yardy*

Nothing dies more quickly than a new idea in a closed mind.

An idea is a funny little thing that won't work unless you do.

Good ideas need landing gear as well as wings. *C. D. Jackson*

Do not follow where the path may lead. Go instead where there is no path, and leave a trail.

The wheel was man's greatest invention until he got behind it.

There is one thing stronger than all the armies in the world, and that is an idea whose time has come. *Victor Hugo*

An inventor is a crackpot who becomes a genius when his idea catches on.

Intelligence

Getting wisdom is the most important
thing you can do! And with your
wisdom, develop common sense
and good judgment.

Proverbs 4:7

Intelligence

A good deal of trouble has been caused in the world by too much intelligence and too little wisdom.

It is not the IQ but the I WILL that is important in education.

Most people have minds like concrete: mixed up and permanently set.

Other people have minds like blotters: They soak up everything but get it all backward.

When most people put in their two cents' worth, they aren't overcharging.

The reason things go in one ear and out the other is that there's nothing to block the traffic.

The problem with second opinions is that that's exactly how long most people think before they offer them.

The mind is like television: When it goes blank it's a good idea to turn off the sound.

Intelligence is like a river—the deeper it is, the less noise it makes.

The reason talk is cheap is that supply far outpaces the demand.

The only reason some people are lost in thought is that they're total strangers there.

Joy

Weeping may go on all night, but in
the morning there is joy.
Psalm 30:5

———

Deceit fills hearts that are plotting
for evil; joy fills hearts that are
planning for good!
Proverbs 12:20

J o y

Joy is the feeling of grinning inside. *Dr. Melba Colgrove*

There is little joy in owning anything that is not shared.

Friendship doubles our joy and divides our grief.

Here are a dozen ways to celebrate joy:

Complete what you start.
Enlarge your interests.
Laugh a lot.
Express gratitude to a friend.
Be kind, thoughtful, and caring.
Read the Bible every day.
Accent the positive.
Tell a friend you love him/her.
Extend a helping hand.
Jot down, every morning, five reasons to be happy.
Overlook pettiness and jealousy.
Yield your life to God.

Grief can take care of itself; but to get the full value of joy, you must have someone to share it with.

The utility company customer with a long-overdue bill claims to have received this rather unusual notice: "We would be delighted if you would pay your bill promptly. If not, you will probably be de-lighted."

Judgment

Getting wisdom is the most important
thing you can do! And with your
wisdom, develop common sense
and good judgment.

Proverbs 4:7

———

Wisdom and good judgment live
together, for wisdom knows where
to discover knowledge and
understanding.

Proverbs 8:12

Judgment

You can't judge another person until you've walked in his shoes.

Judge not a man until you have carried his burdens for twenty-four hours.

God help the sheep when the wolf is judge. *Danish proverb*

Never judge a man by his relatives; he did not choose them.

Never judge a summer resort by its postcards.

You can judge a man not only by the company he keeps but by the jokes he tells.

Why do we judge ourselves by our best intentions and others by their worst faults?

Never judge a man's actions until you know his motives.

You can't always judge a dinner by the price.

The man who has a good opinion of himself is usually a poor judge.

Before judging a sermon, be sure to try it out in practice.

You can judge a man by his enemies as well as by his friends.

Justice

God is more pleased when
we are just and fair than when
we give him gifts.

Proverbs 21:3

Evil men don't understand the
importance of justice, but those who
follow the Lord are much
concerned about it.

Proverbs 28:5

If [kings] drink they may forget their
duties and be unable to give justice to
those who are oppressed.

Proverbs 31:5

Justice

One mouse eats the clothes, and all the mice get into trouble.

Crime's story would be shorter if the sentences were longer.

Those who chronically suffer injustice have the truest insight into what justice is all about.

Fear of the law gives safety.

Justice is truth in action. *Joseph Joubert*

Injustice is relatively easy to bear; what stings is justice.
H. L. Mencken

If a cause is just, it will eventually triumph in spite of all the propaganda issued against it.

Justice without wisdom is impossible. *James Anthony Froude*

The law of the city is the citizens' honor; citizens' sins are a city's disgrace.

Justice delayed is justice denied. *William Gladstone*

Justice is the insurance we have on our property and lives, and obedience is the premium we pay for it.

Justice is the bread of a nation; it is always hungry for it.
François de Chateaubriand

Kindness

Never tire of loyalty and kindness.
Hold these virtues tightly. Write
them deep within your heart.
Proverbs 3:3

———

Your own soul is nourished when
you are kind; it is destroyed
when you are cruel.
Proverbs 11:17

———

The man who tries to be good,
loving, and kind finds life,
righteousness, and honor.
Proverbs 21:21

Kindness

Kindness is something you can't give away, since it always comes back.

Bestow a kindness—then forget it!

Have you had a kindness shown?
Pass it on;
'Twas not given for thee alone,
Pass it on;
Let it travel down the years,
Let it wipe another's tears,
Til in Heaven the deed appears—
Pass it on. *Henry Burton*

Money will buy a fine dog, but only kindness will make him wag his tail.

Kindness is a language that the deaf can hear and the blind can see.

Better is a little kindness while living than an extravagant floral display at the grave.

Kindness consists in loving people more than they deserve. *Joseph Joubert*

The man who raises roses in his garden also does a kindness to his neighbors.

Nothing gives a person more pleasure than doing a good deed in secret and having it found out by accident.

Don't expect to enjoy the cream of life if you keep your milk of human kindness all bottled up.

I expect to pass through the world but once. Any good therefore that I can do, or any kindness that I can show to any fellow creature, let me do it now. Let me not defer it or neglect it, for I shall not pass this way again. *Stephen Grellet (attr.)*

These are three rules of dealing with all those who come to us: (1) Kindness; (2) Kindness; (3) Kindness.
Bishop Fulton J. Sheen

Be kind to everybody. You never know who might show up on the jury at your trial.

The person who sows seeds of kindness will have a perpetual harvest.

One kind word can warm three winter months.
Japanese proverb

Never part without kind words. They might be your last.

Kindness makes a fellow feel good whether it's being done to him or by him. *Frank A. Clark*

Kindness is a warm breeze in a frigid climate, a radiant heat that melts the icebergs of fear, distrust, and unhappiness.

Wise sayings often fall on barren ground, but a kind word is never thrown away. *Sir Arthur Helps*

One can pay back the loan of gold, but one lies forever in debt to those who are kind. *Malay proverb*

Be kind. Remember everyone you meet is fighting a hard battle. *Harry Thompson*

Wherever there is a human being there is a chance for a kindness. *Seneca*

Be kind to people until you make your first million. After that, people will be kind to you.

The kindness we resolve to show tomorrow cures no headache today.

A kind word picks up a man when trouble weighs him down.

Kind words do not wear out the tongue—so speak them.

Knowledge

Wisdom and good judgment live
together, for wisdom knows where
to discover knowledge and
understanding.

Proverbs 8:12

———

The simpleton is crowned with folly;
the wise man is crowned with
knowledge.

Proverbs 14:18

Knowledge

He who knows and knows that he knows, is a master. He who knows and does not know that he knows, needs a teacher. He who does not know and knows that he does know, needs love. He who does not know and knows that he does not know, is lost. *Ancient proverb*

Conceit is what makes a little squirt think he's a fountain of knowledge.

Knowing without doing is like plowing without sowing.

Discussion is an exchange of knowledge; argument is an exchange of ignorance.

Youth: Stay in college; get some knowledge. If God can make penicillin out of moldy bread, he can make something out of you.

A person with a reservoir of knowledge is not well educated unless he knows when to turn the spigot off and on.

You have to know the ropes in order to pull the strings.

The fellow who thinks he is full of knowledge is especially annoying to those of us who are.

Never try to tell everything you know. It may take too short a time. *Norman Ford*

The trouble with the world is not that people know too little, but that they know so many things that ain't so. *Mark Twain*

The road to knowledge begins with the turn of a page.

Laughter

Laughter cannot mask a heavy heart.
When the laughter ends, the
grief remains.
Proverbs 14:13

———

A happy face means a glad heart; a
sad face means a breaking heart.
Proverbs 15:13

Laughter

Laugh a little; it is the hand of God on the shoulder of a troubled world.

Lighten up. Don't sweat the small stuff, and remember, it is all small stuff.

He who laughs, lasts.

On a school bulletin board: "Laugh, and the class laughs with you, but you stay after school alone."

Laughing is the sensation of feeling good all over and showing it principally in one spot. *Josh Billings*

Laughter is the sun that drives winter from the human face. *Victor Hugo*

Laugh at yourself first, before anyone else can. *Elsa Maxwell*

Give me a sense of humor, Lord;
Give me the grace to see a joke,
To get some happiness from life
And pass it on to other folk.

With the fearful strain that is on me night and day, if I did not laugh I should die. *Abraham Lincoln*

Laughter is the brush that sweeps away the cobwebs of the heart. *Mort Walker*

Sit long; talk much; laugh a lot.

Being serious isn't all that important. What counts is knowing what to be serious about.

Laziness

A wise youth makes hay while the sun shines, but what a shame to see a lad who sleeps away his hour of opportunity.

Proverbs 10:5

———

Hard work means prosperity; only a fool idles away his time.

Proverbs 12:11

———

A lazy fellow has trouble all through life; the good man's path is easy!

Proverbs 15:19

Laziness

The man who watches the clock will always be one of the hands.

Laziness travels slowly and is soon overtaken by poverty.

No one ever climbed a hill just by looking at it.

The bee that makes the honey doesn't hang around the hive.

Many people are not failures. They just started at the bottom and like it there.

Fishing is a laborious way of taking it easy.

Doing nothing is the most tiresome job in the world, because you can't stop and rest.

Too many people remind you of French bread—one long loaf.

A new name for laziness is voluntary inertia.

If money grew on trees, some people are so lazy that they wouldn't shake a limb to get it.

The lazier a man is, the more he is going to do tomorrow.

What the world needs is fewer bakers and more delivery boys.

He who rolls up his sleeves seldom loses his shirt.

Leadership

Without wise leadership, a nation
is in trouble; but with good
counselors there is safety.

Proverbs 11:14

———

Work hard and become a leader;
be lazy and never succeed.

Proverbs 12:24

———

When there is moral rot within a
nation, its government topples easily;
but with honest, sensible leaders
there is stability.

Proverbs 28:2

Leadership

What this country needs are more leaders who know what this country needs.

A leader does the right thing; a manager does the thing right.

Either lead, follow, or get out of the way. *Ted Turner*

He who is not afraid to face the music may sometime lead the band.

You do not lead by hitting people over the head—that's assault, not leadership. *Dwight Eisenhower*

Anyone can steer the ship when the sea is calm.

He who cannot obey, cannot command. *Benjamin Franklin*

Leadership is the courage to admit mistakes, the vision to welcome change, the enthusiasm to motivate others, and the confidence to stay out of step when everyone else is marching to the wrong tune. *E. M. Estes*

All the roads to success and achievement are uphill.

A truly great leader is one who never allows his followers to discover that he is as ignorant as they are.

Learning

How does a man become wise? The first step is to trust and reverence the Lord! Only fools refuse to be taught. Listen to your father and mother. What you learn from them will stand you in good stead; it will gain you many honors.

Proverbs 1:7-9

To learn, you must want to be taught. To refuse reproof is stupid.

Proverbs 12:1

Learning

Learn from the skillful; he who teaches himself has a fool for a master.

The only things worth learning are the things you learn after you know it all. *Harry S. Truman*

What people fail to learn from sermons they later learn from experience.

Learning is like rowing upstream; not to advance is to drop back.

Reading makes a full man; conference, a ready man; and writing, an exact man. *Francis Bacon*

He who graduates today, and stops learning tomorrow, is uneducated the day after. *Newton D. Baker*

It was Junior's first day in school, and when he got home his mother asked, "Did you learn anything today?"
"No," he replied in disgust. "I have to go back tomorrow."

Learn from the mistakes of others. You won't live long enough to make them all yourself.

A college education never hurt anybody who was willing to learn after he got it.

Life and Death

For whoever finds [Wisdom] finds life
and wins approval from the Lord. . . .
Those who refuse [Wisdom] show
that they love death.

Proverbs 8:35-36

The good man finds life;
the evil man, death.

Proverbs 11:19

The path of the godly leads to life.
So why fear death?

Proverbs 12:28

Life and Death

Living is like licking honey off a thorn. *Louis Adamic*

Most of the shadows of this life are caused by standing in one's own sunshine. *Ralph Waldo Emerson*

Let us endeavor to so live that when we come to die even the undertaker will be sorry. *Mark Twain*

Life's greatest tragedy is to lose God and not to miss him. *F. W. Norwood*

Did you hear about the undertaker who closed his letters with the words, "Eventually yours"?

The man who strays away from common sense will end up dead! *Proverbs 21:16*

Death—the poor man's doctor. *German proverb*

I know of nobody who has a mind to die this year. *William Shakespeare*

It is important that when we come to die we have nothing to do but to die. *Charles Hodge*

When an evil man dies, his hopes all perish, for they are based upon this earthly life. *Proverbs 11:7*

Love

Young man, do not resent it when God
chastens and corrects you, for his
punishment is proof of his love.

Proverbs 3:11

Hatred stirs old quarrels, but
love overlooks insults.

Proverbs 10:12

Love forgets mistakes; nagging about
them parts the best of friends.

Proverbs 17:9

Love

Love is a feeling that makes a woman make a man make a fool of himself.

Life is just one fool thing after another; love is just two fool things after each other.

Indifference, not hate, is the strongest enemy of love.
C. S. Lewis

He loves each one of us as if there were only one of us.
St. Augustine

Love God completely; love others compassionately; love yourself correctly.

Love—what you keep to yourself you lose; what you give away you keep forever.

Money can build a house, but it takes love to make it a home.

And love in the heart wasn't put there to stay;
Love isn't love 'till you give it away. *Oscar Hammerstein II*

A husband knows his wife loves him when she returns a dress he can't afford.

He who falls in love with himself will have no rivals.

Love makes the lonelies go away.

Love is the glue that cements friendship; jealousy keeps it from sticking.

Nothing beats love at first sight except love with insight.

On an average day, 3,502 fifth graders fall in love.

Sign in an airline office: "God loves you, and I'm trying to."

Love cures people—both the ones that give it and the ones who receive it. *Dr. Karl Menninger*

Love demands all, and has a right to do it. *Beethoven*

Love and eggs are best when they are fresh. *Russian proverb*

Perfect love sometimes does not come 'till the first grandchild. *Saul Bellow*

Many a man in love with a dimple makes the mistake of marrying the whole girl. *Stephen Leacock*

Love has been described as a five-ring circus: First comes the telephone ring, then the engagement ring, then the wedding ring, then the teething ring, and after that the suffer-ring.

Faults are thick where love is thin. *James Howell*

Eve: Adam, do you love me?
Adam: Who else?

We flatter those we scarcely know,
We please the fleeting guest,
And deal full many a thoughtless blow
To those we love the best. *Ella Wheeler Wilcox*

Love is an ocean of emotions, entirely surrounded by expenses. *Thomas R. Dewar*

A practical nurse is one who falls in love with a wealthy patient.

Puppy love is just a prelude to a dog's life.

The most important thing a father can do for his children is love their mother.

Love at first sight is often cured by a second look.

Love is like a vaccination—when it takes hold, you don't have to be told.

Man/Husband

The man who knows right from wrong
and has good judgment and common
sense is happier than the man
who is immensely rich! For such
wisdom is far more valuable than
precious jewels. Nothing else
compares with it.
Proverbs 3:13-15

Man / Husband

Man blames fate for other accidents, but feels personally responsible when he makes a hole-in-one.

Speaker being introduced at civic club luncheon: "I've known him as a man, as an adolescent, and as a child—sometimes all in the same day!"

Many a man wishes he were as smart as his wife thinks he is.

Man—that inconsistent creation who is always insisting on hotel service around home and home environment at hotels.

Most men need two women in their lives—a secretary to take everything down, and a wife to pick everything up.

Man—a living creature who buys football tickets three months in advance and waits until Christmas Eve to do his gift shopping.

Self-made men should be more careful in selecting the material they use.

The best thing some self-made men could do is deny it.

What the average man wants to get out of his new car is the kids.

Humility is usually one of the qualities left out of the self-made man.

The average man is able to detect a rattle in his car more quickly than one in his head.

Marriage

Drink from your own well, my son—be faithful and true to your wife. Be happy, yes, rejoice in the wife of your youth.

Proverbs 5:15, 18

The man who finds a wife finds a good thing; she is a blessing to him from the Lord.

Proverbs 18:22

Marriage

Marry in haste, and repent at leisure.

Did you hear about the couple who got married at an early urge?

Those who hope for a happy marriage will do well to remember that in *wedding* the *we* comes before the *I.*

I have learned that only two things are necessary to keep one's wife happy. First, let her think she is having her way. And second, let her have it. *Lyndon B. Johnson*

After a few years of marriage a man can look right at a woman without seeing her, and a woman can see right through a man without looking at him.

Women who henpeck their husbands are apt to find them with other chicks.

A man who gives in when he is wrong is wise. A man who gives in when he is right is married.

Success in marriage is not so much a matter of finding the right person as it is *being* the right person.

Troubles in marriage often start when a man is so busy earning his salt that he forgets his sugar.

Even when a marriage is made in heaven, the maintenance work has to be done here on earth.

Many a domestic explosion has been touched off by an old flame.

Woman to marriage counselor: "That's my side of the story—now let me tell you his."

Psychiatrists say girls tend to marry men like their fathers. Now we know why mothers cry at weddings.

Marriage occurs when a man gets hooked on his own line.

Epitaph: Here lies my darling husband, Walter. May he rest in peace until we meet again.

Successful marriage is always a triangle: a man, a woman, and God.

Marriage is like a meal in which the dessert is the first course.

A husband is a diplomat who remembers his wife's birthday but not her age.

The modern husband too often comes home from work and greets his wife: "Hiya, honey, what's thawing?"

Adam and Eve had an ideal marriage. He didn't have to hear about all the men she could have married, and she didn't hear about how well his mother cooked.

There are two periods in a man's life when he doesn't understand women—before and after marriage.

When a man and woman marry, they become one. The trouble starts when they try to decide which one.

If you are a child of God and you marry a child of the devil, you will be sure to have constant trouble with your father-in-law.

It takes at least two people to make a marriage—a single girl and an anxious mother.

The trouble with marriage is not the institution—it's personnel.

A good many things are easier said than done—including the marriage ceremony.

A marriage may be holy wedlock or unholy deadlock.

To marry a woman for her beauty is like buying a house for its paint.

The bonds of matrimony are worthless unless the interest is kept up.

Romance goes out the window when she stops knitting and starts needling.

Another thing marriage brings out in a lot of men is silence.

What a married couple should save for their old age is each other.

The most impressive evidence of tolerance is a golden wedding anniversary.

The only state that permits a woman to work more than eight hours a day is the state of matrimony.

A successful marriage is one in which you fall in love many times, always with the same person. *D. W. McLaughlin*

Doing housework for thirty dollars a day is domestic service; doing it for nothing is matrimony.

Mercy

It is only the Lord's mercies that have
kept us from complete destruction.

Lamentations 3:22

Mercy

Sign tacked on a tree near a convent: "No trespassing; violators will be prosecuted to the fullest extent of the law—Sisters of Mercy."

Among the attributes of God, although they are all equal, mercy shines with even more brilliance than justice.

God's wrath comes by measure; his mercy without measure.

We hand folks over to God's mercy, and show none ourselves. *George Eliot*

Who will not mercy on others show, How can he mercy ever hope to have? *Edmund Spenser*

Mistakes

A wise man controls his temper. He
knows that anger causes mistakes.

Proverbs 14:29

———

God will help the king to judge
the people fairly; there need
be no mistakes.

Proverbs 16:10

———

Love forgets mistakes; nagging about
them parts the best of friends.

Proverbs 17:9

Mistakes

To get maximum attention, it's hard to beat a big mistake.

He who takes the wrong road makes the journey twice.

The biggest fool of all is the person who refuses to profit by his mistakes.

The man who boasts that he never made a mistake has a wife who did.

Don't worry about your mistakes. Some of the dullest people don't make *any*.

Our God has a big eraser.

The man who never makes a mistake must get tired of doing nothing.

A mistake proves that someone at least tried.

Most people would learn from their mistakes if they weren't so busy trying to place the blame on someone else.

He who makes a mistake and doesn't correct it is making another mistake.

If you don't learn from your mistakes, there's no sense in making them.

Money

Trust in your money and down
you go! Trust in God and
flourish as a tree.
Proverbs 11:28

———

The wise man saves for the future,
but the foolish man spends
whatever he gets.
Proverbs 21:20

———

Don't weary yourself trying to get
rich. Why waste your time? For riches
can disappear as though they had
the wings of a bird!
Proverbs 23:4-5

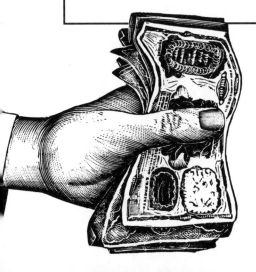

Money

Make all you can, save all you can, give all you can.
John Wesley

Being kidnapped and held for ransom never worries the poor
man! *Proverbs 13:8*

A penny goes a long way today. You can carry it around for
weeks before you find something you can buy with it.

When a person has money to burn, you can be sure somebody
will be around to hand him a match.

By the time a man discovers that money doesn't grow on
trees, he's already way out on a limb. *Cy N. Peace*

A dollar may not go as far as it used to, but what it lacks in dis-
tance it makes up in speed.

For you can't take it with you,
They've told me for years,
And I've wisdom enough to perceive it.
What's more, from the way that
It's going, I doubt
That I'll even be able to leave it.

Money can't buy you friends, but it can bring you a better
class of enemies.

Miser: one who's perfectly content to let the rest of the world
go buy.

When we were kids, ten cents was big money. How dimes have
changed!

One of the benefits of inflation is that the kids can no longer get sick on a nickel's worth of candy.

Many Americans seem to feel that living within their income is a fate worse than debt.

A collection has been defined as a church function in which many take a passing interest.

Sign in a store window: "This is a nonprofit organization—please help us change."

Money used to talk; then it whispered; now it just sneaks off.

One reason they put men's faces on money is that women are satisfied just to get their hands on it.

Husband, looking over the bills, to wife: "Well, we're at the bridge we were going to cross when we came to it."

To satisfy the itch for money, scratch for it!

Speaking of money, it doesn't make you completely happy—but it sure quiets the nerves.

A hat was passed around a certain congregation for a guest minister. When it was returned to the parson, it was emphatically and embarrassingly empty. Slowly and deliberately the parson inverted the hat and shook it meaningfully. Then, raising his eyes to heaven, he exclaimed fervently: "I thank Thee, dear Lord, that I got my hat back from this congregation."

Funny how ten dollars looks so big when you take it to church and so small when you take it to the store.

Money talks, but it doesn't say when it's coming back.

Woman to neighbor: "My economic philosophy is middle-of-the-road. I spend money left and right."

The man who marries for money will earn it.

Why do we spend twenty thousand dollars on a school bus to haul our children one mile and then build a five-million-dollar gymnasium for them to get exercise?

Probably the world's greatest humorist was the man who named them "easy payments."

Money can buy a bed, but not rest; food, but not satisfaction; luxury, but not contentment.

Money won't buy happiness, but it will pay the salaries of a large research staff to study the problem.

Don't marry for money; you can borrow it more cheaply.

If you had your life to live over again, you'd need more money.

Money isn't everything, but it sure keeps you in touch with the children.

The nice thing about a gift of money is that it's so easy to exchange.

Every time you lend money to a friend you damage his memory.

I should like to leave a poor man with a great deal of money.
Pablo Picasso

By the time you have money to burn, the fire has gone out.

No horse goes as fast as the money people put on it.

Money is a good servant but a poor master.

He who is quick on the draw has little left in the checking account.

A new car isn't a sign of how much money a fellow has, but it's a pretty good indication of how much he owes.

There are a lot of hot arguments over cold cash.

What do atheists do with their money? Surely they wouldn't carry around anything that says "In God We Trust."

The thing a little boy outgrows fastest is his allowance.

By the time a man can afford to buy one of those little sports cars, he's too fat to get into it.

A family budget is a device to make you worry about money *before* you spend it.

Many people hate change—unless it jingles in their pockets.

A person's character is put to the test when he suddenly acquires or quickly loses a considerable amount of money.

Christmas is a race to see which gives out first—your money or your feet.

On Christmas Eve Santa carries the bag. After Christmas, Dad and Mom are holding it.

Separation of church and state could hardly be more complete. The church teaches that money isn't everything, and the government keeps telling us it is.

Nothing makes a woman's clothes go out of style faster than a raise in salary.

Contentment occurs when your earning power equals your yearning power.

The exercise that wears most people out is running after cash.

Mother

Don't despise an old mother's
experience.

Proverbs 23:22

———

Listen to your father and mother.
What you learn from them will stand
you in good stead; it will gain
you many honors.

Proverbs 1:8-9

Mother

The father is the head of the house; the mother is the heart of the house.

Simply having children does not make mothers.

God could not be everywhere, so he invented mothers.
Hebrew proverb

Just about the time a mother thinks her work is done, she becomes a grandmother.

Mothers write on the hearts of their children what the world's rough hand cannot erase.

There is no modern pain medicine as effective as a mother's kiss.

If one wants to see genuine beauty, he will find it in the tender lines that sacrificial love has drawn upon a mother's face.

An ounce of mother is worth a pound of clergy.
Spanish proverb

A man is seldom as smart as his mother thinks, or as dumb as his mother-in-law says he is.

Another reason for unhappy marriages is that men can't fool their wives like they could their mothers.

All mothers are physically handicapped. They have only two hands.

Let France have good mothers, and she will have good sons. *Napoléon Bonaparte*

If we want to change our nation, begin by enlisting the mothers. *Sir Winston Churchill*

All that I am, or hope to be, I owe to my angel mother. *Abraham Lincoln*

The future destiny of the child is always the work of the mother. *Napoléon Bonaparte*

Virtues are learned at Mother's knee—vices at some other joint.

The joys of motherhood are never fully experienced until all the children are in bed.

Young mother to a friend: "He's eating solids now—keys, bits of paper, pencils . . ."

The greatest teacher I ever had was my mother. *George Washington*

Any mother could perform the jobs of several traffic-controllers with ease. *Lisa Alther*

Mothers understand what children do not say. *Jewish proverb*

One mother achieves more than a hundred teachers.

Many a man met his wife through a dating service—her mother!

The young mother gets along beautifully with her mother-in-law because she probably can't afford a baby-sitter.

Wife: "What are you getting my mother for her birthday this year?"
Husband: "A cemetery lot."
ONE YEAR LATER
Wife: "What are you getting my mother for her birthday this year?"
Husband: "Nothing! She didn't use what I got her last year."

The penalty for bigamy is two mothers-in-law.

No man is really successful until his mother-in-law admits it.

What a mother should save for a rainy day is patience.

Motivation

We can justify our every deed, but
God looks at our motives.

Proverbs 21:2

———

Choose [Wisdom's] instruction
instead of silver, . . . for wisdom
is more precious than rubies,
and nothing you desire can
compare with her.

Proverbs 8:10-11, NIV

———

The one thing I want from God, the
thing I seek most of all, is the
privilege of meditating in his Temple,
lilving in his presence every day of
my life, delighting in his
incomparable perfections and glory.

Psalm 27:4

Motivation

In winter, the big problem is how to get seventy-two inches of son to shovel three and a half inches of snow.

One motivation is worth ten threats, two pressures, and six reminders. *Paul Sweeney*

Other people see your deeds. God sees your motives.

Coaches who can outline plays on a blackboard are a dime a dozen. The ones who win get inside their players and motivate. *Vince Lombardi*

Six-thirty is my time to rise,
But I'm seldom bright of eye;
Part of me says, "Look alive!"
And the other part asks, "Why?"

Whatever you do, work at it with all your heart, as working for the Lord, not for men. *Colossians 3:23, NIV*

Motivation is what gets you started. Habit is what keeps you going. *Jim Ryun*

People are always motivated for at least two reasons: the one they tell you about, and a secret one. *O. A. Battista*

He that does good for God's sake seeks neither praise nor reward; he is sure of both in the end. *William Penn*

Mouth/Speech

Don't talk so much. You keep putting
your foot in your mouth. Be sensible
and turn off the flow.

Proverbs 10:19

———

A fool gets into constant fights.
His mouth is his undoing!
His words endanger him.

Proverbs 18:6-7

Mouth/Speech

He who thinks by the inch and talks by the yard deserves to be kicked by the foot.

It isn't hard to make a mountain out of a molehill; just add a little dirt.

Some teens' mouths are so big, there's room for another set of teeth.

A closed mouth gathers no feet.

As the momma whale said to the baby whale, "It's only when you're spouting that you get harpooned."

The best way to save face is to keep the lower part shut.

Language is the dress of thought; every time you open your mouth your mind is on parade.

Be sure your brain is in gear before engaging your mouth.

She who has the gift of gab doesn't know how to wrap it up.

A wise old owl lived in an oak;
The more he saw, the less he spoke;
The less he spoke, the more he heard;
Why can't we all be like that bird?

Obedience

Obey me and live! Guard my words
as your most precious possession.
Write them down, and also keep them
deep within your heart.

Proverbs 7:2-3

Despise God's Word and find yourself
in trouble. Obey it and succeed.

Proverbs 13:13

God blesses those who obey him;
happy the man who puts his
trust in the Lord.

Proverbs 16:20

Obedience

He who has learned to obey will know how to command.
William Arthur Ward

Every great person first learned how to obey, whom to obey, and when to obey.

Who says kids aren't obedient? They'll obey any TV commercial about buying a new toy.

The time to teach obedience to authority is in the playpen instead of the state pen.

Obedience is the mother of success, and is wedded to safety.
Thomas à Kempis

Delayed obedience is the brother of disobedience.

Christ was one child who knew more than his parents—yet he obeyed them.

The Christian who claims the promises of God should also obey the commands of God.

God's laws last longer than those who break them.

Obedience to God removes pretense from our prayers.

The cost of obedience is nothing compared with the cost of disobedience.

A patient cannot accept the physician and, at the same time, reject his remedy.

Opportunity

A wise youth makes hay while the sun
shines, but what a shame to see a lad
who sleeps away his hour
of opportunity.

Proverbs 10:5

Opportunity

An opportunist pulls himself up by your bootstraps.
Al Bernstein

Today's opportunity is yesterday's dream and tomorrow's memory.

The older you get, the longer it takes to get to the door if opportunity knocks.

There's something in life that never returns—a lost opportunity!

The only difference between stumbling blocks and stepping-stones is the way you use them.

He who says the days of opportunity are over is copping out.

Opportunity is missed by most people because it is dressed in overalls and looks like work. ***Thomas Edison***

Four things never come back—the spoken word, the sped arrow, the past life, and the neglected opportunity.
Arab proverb

Gentlemen, we're surrounded by insurmountable opportunities. ***Pogo***

I'll study and get ready and be prepared for my opportunity when it comes. ***Abraham Lincoln***

Optimism/Pessimism

The wicked man's fears will all come
true and so will the good man's hopes.

Proverbs 10:24

———

There is a right time for everything.

Ecclesiastes 3:1

Optimism/Pessimism

Optimists are people who get wealthy by buying out pessimists.

An optimist invented the boat; a pessimist invented the life preserver.

Pessimists break mirrors just to make sure they live another seven years.

Pessimists burn all their bridges ahead of them.

A hopeless pessimist is always building dungeons in the air.

A pessimist is someone who feels bad when he feels good for fear he'll feel worse when he feels better. *Thomas Jefferson*

An optimist is a fellow who double-parks while his wife steps into the store for a "moment."

If it weren't for the optimist, the pessimist would never know how happy he isn't.

An optimist may be wrong, but he bears mistakes with fortitude.

A pessimist is a person who looks at the world through woes-colored glasses.

Pessimists always take the cynic route. *Antoni Tabok*

Optimists are nostalgic about the future.

An optimist is a person who is a hope addict.

The optimist has no brakes; the pessimist has no motor.

When confronted with a Goliath-size problem, which way do you respond—"He's too big to hit," or, like David, "He's too big to miss"?

He who sees an enemy behind every tree is a pessimist.

An optimist is a fellow who believes a housefly is looking for a way to get out. *George Nathan*

The pessimist sees the difficulty in every opportunity; the optimist sees the opportunity in every difficulty. *L. P. Jacks*

Some people are making such thorough plans for rainy days that they aren't enjoying today's sunshine. *William Feather*

No matter how bright the sunshine, pious pessimists point to the tunnel at the end of the light.

The optimist is often as wrong as the pessimist, but he is far happier.

An optimist is always broke.

An optimist is a guy who tells you to cheer up when things are going his way.

The optimist fell ten stories. At each floor he shouted to his friend, "All right so far!"

An optimist builds castles in the sky. A dreamer lives there. A realist collects rent from both of them.

An optimist is one who, instead of feeling sorry he cannot pay his bills, is glad he is not one of his creditors.

An optimist says his glass is still half full; a pessimist declares that his glass is already half empty.

Optimism is a cheerful frame of mind that enables a teakettle to sing though in hot water up to its neck.

Keep your face to the sunshine and you cannot see the shadow. *Helen Keller*

A pessimist says that anytime things appear to be going better, you have overlooked something.

You know it's going to be a bad week when your boss mails you want ads.

A pessimist always looks both ways when he crosses a one-way street.

Always borrow from a pessimist; he never expects to get it back.

An optimist is one who makes the best of it when he gets the worst of it.

Parents

Listen to your father's advice
and don't despise an old mother's
experience. . . . The father of a
godly man has cause for joy—what
pleasure a wise son is! So give
your parents joy!
Proverbs 23:22, 24-25

———

A man who robs his parents and says,
"What's wrong with that?" is no
better than a murderer.
Proverbs 28:24

Parents

"Sparents" are those who spare the rod
When offspring need attention;
They find their troubles multiplied
In ways too sad to mention.

If you have teenagers in your house, you'll find it difficult to understand how farmers could possibly grow a surplus of food.

Note on church bulletin board: "Parents, be the soul support of your children."

The reason some parents no longer lead their children in the right direction is that they aren't going that way themselves.

No wonder it's tough to be a teenager. Half the grown-ups tell him to find himself, and the other half tell him to get lost!

When my father found me on the wrong track, he always provided switching facilities.

It's foolish to worry about confused teenagers. Give them time and they'll grow up to be confused adults!

Next year 4 million kids will turn sixteen, and 8 million parents will turn pale.

One reason so many children are seen on the streets at night is that they're afraid to stay home alone.

A diplomat is a parent with two boys on different Little League teams.

You really believe in heredity when your child's report card is all A's.

Parents who are afraid to put their foot down usually have children who step on their toes.

Some parents are not on "spanking terms" with their children.

The behavior of some children suggests that their parents embarked on the sea of matrimony without a paddle.

Many children would take after their parents if they knew where they went.

The parents gave their daughter a new car as a birthday present. On the windshield was a card signed, "With all our love, Mama and Pauper."

A real family man is one who can look at his new child as an addition rather than a deduction.

Some parents can trace their ancestry back three hundred years, but they cannot tell where their children were last night.

The trouble with being a parent is that by the time we're experienced, we're unemployed.

Far too often, rich parents are poor parents.

Parents can tell but never teach, until they practice what they preach.

The accent may be on youth, but the stress is still on the parents.

Really, the younger generation isn't so bad. It's just that they have more critics than models.

Adolescence occurs when children start bringing up their parents.

Parents are the last people on earth who ought to have children. *Samuel Butler*

Train up a child in the way he should go—and walk there yourself once in a while. *Josh Billings*

Do not handicap your children by making their lives easy. *Robert Heinlein*

We never know the love of the parent till we become parents ourselves. *Henry Ward Beecher*

Parents wonder why the streams are bitter, when they themselves have poisoned the fountain. *John Locke*

When our parents are living, we feel that they stand between us and death; when they are gone, we ourselves are in the forefront of the battle.

Just about the time you think your problems are all behind you, you become a grandparent.

The most important thing a father can do for his children is love their mother.

Persistence

Steady plodding brings prosperity;
hasty speculation brings poverty.

Proverbs 21:5

———

O evil man, leave the upright man
alone and quit trying to cheat him
out of his rights. Don't you know that
this good man, though you trip him
up seven times, will each time rise
again? But one calamity is
enough to lay you low.

Proverbs 24:15-16

Persistence

Failure is the path of least persistence.

I'm a slow walker, but I never walk back. *Abraham Lincoln*

Wealthy people miss one of life's greatest pleasures—making the last payment.

By perseverance, the snail reached the ark. *Charles Spurgeon*

The man who removes a mountain begins by carrying away small stones. *Chinese proverb*

Life is hard,
By the yard;
But by the inch,
Life's a cinch!
Jean L. Gordon

When William Carey was asked the reason for his success as a missionary, he replied, "I can plod."

Consider the postage stamp: Its usefulness consists in the ability to stick to one thing till it gets there. *Josh Billings*

Stopping at third base adds no more to the score than striking out.

Stick to your job until one of you is finished.

Paralyze resistance with persistence. *Woody Hayes*

Perseverance has been defined as sticking to something you're not stuck on.

Plans

It is pleasant to see plans develop.
That is why fools refuse to give
them up even when they are wrong.
Proverbs 13:19

———

We can make our plans, but the final
outcome is in God's hands.
Proverbs 16:1

———

We should make plans—counting
on God to direct us.
Proverbs 16:9

Plans

He who aims at nothing is sure to hit it.

Plan ahead—it wasn't raining when Noah built the ark!

Light your lamp before night overtakes you.

What is planned ahead of time can be done quickly.

He who plans his program for tomorrow takes confusion out of the day.

When you fail to plan, you plan to fail.

Make long-range plans as if you are going to live forever, and live today as if it were your last day on earth.

God has no problems—only plans. *Corrie ten Boom*

The plans are man's; the odds are God's.

One of the greatest things about life is not so much where we stand as what direction we are going.

Don't brag about your plans for tomorrow—wait and see what happens. *Proverbs 27:1*

He who lays no plans for the future will have an empty old age.

Hang your basket where you can reach it.

When you're dying of thirst, it's too late to think about digging a well. *Japanese proverb*

Prayer

The Lord hates the gifts of the wicked
but delights in the prayers
of his people.
Proverbs 15:8

———

The Lord is far from the wicked,
but he hears the prayers
of the righteous.
Proverbs 15:29

Prayer

Women are always involved in spiritual affairs. All of the women I ever asked out said that I didn't have a prayer.
Bob Hope

Notice on high school bulletin board: "In the event of nuclear attack, all bans on prayer on this campus will be lifted."

Courage is fear that has said its prayers.

Prayer is the stop that keeps you going.

If your knees are knocking, kneel on them.

You're on your toes when you're on your knees.

Did you hear about the two small schoolboys who were sitting in the corner facing the wall?
"What are you here for?" one asked.
"I got caught talking to Joy! What about you?"
"I got caught talking to God!"

Now there's even a "dial-a-prayer" for atheists. You call a number and nobody answers.

Many prayers go to heaven's dead-letter office for want of sufficient direction.

True prayer is a way of life, not just in case of an emergency.

Give your troubles to God; he'll be up all night anyway.

Life is fragile—handle with prayer.

Who goes to bed and does not pray, maketh two nights to every day. *George Herbert*

If your day is hemmed with prayer, it is less likely to unravel.

A prayer in its simplest definition is really a wish turned Godward.

There will always be prayers in public schools—as long as there are final exams to take. *B. Norman Frisch*

Do not pray for easy lives. Pray to be stronger men. Do not pray for tasks commensurate with your strength. Pray for strength commensurate with your tasks. *Phillips Brooks*

What isn't won in prayer first, is never won at all. *Malcolm Cronk*

If God shuts one door, he opens another. *Irish proverb*

Prayer is the key of the morning and the bolt of the night.

He who cannot reach the mission field on his feet can reach it on his knees.

At the close of catechism class, a twelve-year-old girl was called to pray. Said she, "O Lord, thank you for all you've done, and keep up the good work."

Every step in the progress of missions is directly traceable to prayer. It has been the preparation for every new triumph and the secret for all success. *A. T. Pierson*

When praying, don't give God instructions. God listens to prayer, not advice.

A teenager's view of prayer: "There are four answers to prayer—yes, no, wait awhile, and you've got to be kidding!"

Before we can pray, "Thy Kingdom come," we must be willing to pray, "My kingdom go." *Alan Redpath*

If God is your Father, please call home.

Many a man kept going straight because his mother bent her knees in prayer.

Many a fellow is praying for rain with his bucket wrong side up.

He who is a stranger to prayer is a stranger to power.

When I pray, coincidences happen, and when I don't, they don't.

Seven days without prayer makes one weak.

More things are wrought by prayer than this world dreams of. *Alfred, Lord Tennyson*

The man who says his prayers in the evening is a captain posting his sentries. After that, he can sleep. *Charles Baudelaire*

He who spreads the sails of prayer will eventually fly the flag of praise.

Pray hardest when it is hardest to pray. Prayer is a powerful thing, for God has bound and tied himself thereto. *Martin Luther*

The one concern of the devil is to keep Christians from praying. He fears nothing from prayerless studies, prayerless works, and prayerless religion. He laughs at our toil, mocks at wisdom, but trembles when we pray. *Samuel Chadwick*

Nothing lies beyond the reach of prayer except that which lies outside the will of God.

He who is swept off his feet needs to get on his knees.

He who runs from God in the morning will scarcely find him the rest of the day. *John Bunyan*

A Christian sees more on his knees than a philosopher on his tiptoes.

Pray to God, but row toward the shore. *Russian proverb*

Sign outside a Dallas church: "Last chance to pray before entering the freeway."

Behind every work of God you will always find some kneeling form. *Dwight L. Moody*

He who says he is an atheist has no one to talk to when he is alone.

He who would be respected must be fervent in his prayer, fearless in his principles, firm in his purposes, and faithful in his promises.

Prayers can't be answered unless they are prayed.

Satan trembles when he sees the weakest saint upon his knees. *William Cowper*

He stands best who kneels most; he stands strongest who kneels weakest; he stands longest who kneels lowest. Bent knees mean strong backs.

He who tunes up in the morning stays in harmony all day.

Sign in front of a church: "Our church is prayer-conditioned."

Even the feeblest knock is heard on heaven's door.

I have been driven many times to my knees by the overwhelming conviction that I had nowhere else to go. My own wisdom, and that of all about me, seemed insufficient for the day.
Abraham Lincoln

Life's road is rough, but you can make it; hold out your hand, and God will take it.

When we work, we work; when we pray, God works.

Preparation

Go ahead and prepare for the conflict,
but victory comes from God.
Proverbs 21:31

A prudent man foresees the
difficulties ahead and
prepares for them.
Proverbs 22:3

Any enterprise is built by wise
planning, becomes strong through
common sense, and profits
wonderfully by keeping
abreast of the facts.
Proverbs 24:3-4

Preparation

Failure to prepare is preparing to fail. *John Wooden*

He who has not prepared for the trip should not begin his journey.

To be prepared for war is one of the most effectual means of preserving peace. *George Washington*

Don't cross the bridge until you have the exact toll ready.

A Brownie leader asked her group, "What is the Girl Scout motto?" "Be repaired," piped one little miss.

The past is valuable to you as a guidepost, but dangerous if used as a hitching post.

Luck is what happens when preparation meets opportunity. *Elmer Letterman*

The time to repair the roof is when the sun is shining. *John F. Kennedy*

Today's preparation determines tomorrow's achievement.

Change favors the prepared mind. *Louis Pasteur*

Successful salesmanship is 90 percent preparation and 10 percent presentation.

There are four steps to accomplishment: Plan purposely. Prepare prayerfully. Proceed positively. Pursue persistently.

Pride

Proud men end in shame, but the
meek become wise.

Proverbs 11:2

———

If you have been a fool by being
proud or plotting evil, don't brag
about it—cover your mouth
with your hand in shame.

Proverbs 30:32

Pride

Pride is the only disease that everyone around you suffers from except yourself.

Pride breakfasted with plenty, dined with poverty, and supped with infamy. *Benjamin Franklin*

Swallow your pride occasionally, and console yourself with the knowledge that it is 100 percent calorie free.

The proud man counts his newspaper clippings—the humble man his blessings. *Bishop Fulton J. Sheen*

A sure cure for conceit and pride is a visit to the cemetery, where eggheads and boneheads get equal billing.

Pride goes before destruction and haughtiness before a fall. Better poor and humble than proud and rich. *Proverbs 16:18-19*

When you know you've got humility, you've lost it. Humility is to make a right estimate of one's self. *Charles Spurgeon*

Be humble or you'll stumble. *Dwight L. Moody*

Problems

"I want to make the simpleminded
wise!" [Solomon] said. "I want to
warn young men about some
problems they will face."

Proverbs 1:4

———

A sensible man watches for problems
ahead and prepares to meet them. The
simpleton never looks and suffers
the consequences.

Proverbs 27:12

Problems

Some people approach every problem with an open mouth. *Adlai Stevenson*

A problem well stated is a problem half resolved. *Charles F. Kettering*

Problems shouldn't be faced; they should be attacked.

In this Book [the Bible] will be found the solution of all the problems of the world. *Calvin Coolidge*

Every problem is a possibility in disguise.

God has no problems, only plans. *Corrie ten Boom*

Our problems should make us better, not bitter.

The problem is that the key to success doesn't always fit your ignition.

You've got a problem when your dentist tells you that you need a bridge and you can't pay his toll.

Sign on the chaplain's desk: "If you have problems, tell me about them. If you don't, tell me how you do it."

If you could kick the fellow responsible for most of your problems, you wouldn't be able to sit down for a month!

Be thankful for your problems, for if they were less difficult, someone with less ability would have your job.

If only men took the nation's problems as seriously as they do its sports!

Promises

God delights in those who keep their
promises and abhors those who don't.
Proverbs 12:22

It is foolish and rash to make
a promise to the Lord before
counting the cost.
Proverbs 20:25

One who doesn't give the gift he
promised is like a cloud blowing over
a desert without dropping any rain.
Proverbs 25:14

Promises

He who thinks by the inch and talks by the yard deserves to be kicked by the foot.

The politician was full of promises that went in one year and out the other.

The promises of God are certain, but they do not all mature in ninety days. *Adoniram J. Gordon*

You can fix anything but a broken promise.

He who is the slowest in making a promise is the most faithful in keeping it.

Don't put a promise in my ear; put it in my hand. *Russian proverb*

You can never break God's promises by leaning on them.

God's promises are like the stars; the darker the night, the brighter they shine.

God didn't promise an easy voyage, but a safe arrival.

Quarrels

To quarrel with a neighbor is foolish;
a man with good sense
holds his tongue.

Proverbs 11:12

———

It is hard to stop a quarrel once it
starts, so don't let it begin.

Proverbs 17:14

———

The selfish man quarrels against
every sound principle of conduct
by demanding his own way.

Proverbs 18:1

Quarrels

Never pick a quarrel—even when it's ripe.

Very often a fight for what is right turns into a quarrel over what is left.

Perhaps the only way to avoid quarreling with your wife is to let her go her way and you go hers.

There are usually two sides to every argument but no end.

When arguing with a stupid person, be sure he isn't doing the same thing.

Arguments provide plenty of heat but little light.

The only way to get the best of an argument is to avoid it.
Dale Carnegie

When one will not, two cannot quarrel.

A quarrel is like buttermilk. The longer it stands, the more sour it becomes.

Quarrels would never last long if there were not faults on both sides. *La Rochefoucauld*

Those who in quarrels interpose, must often wipe a bloody nose. *Benjamin Franklin*

A quarrelsome man has no good neighbors.
Benjamin Franklin

Quietness

A gossip goes around spreading
rumors, while a trustworthy man
tries to quiet them.

Proverbs 11:13

———

The man of few words and settled
mind is wise; therefore, even a
fool is thought to be wise when
he is silent. It pays him to
keep his mouth shut.

Proverbs 17:27-28

Quietness

I have never been hurt by anything I didn't say.
Calvin Coolidge

Silence is evidence of a superb command of the English language.

I regret often that I have spoken; never that I have been silent.
Syrus

Conversation enriches the understanding, but solitude is the school of genius. *Edward Gibbon*

If silence is golden, not many people could be accused of hoarding.

Radio announcer: "The three minutes of quietness on your radio, ladies and gentlemen, was not due to technical difficulties but was brought to you through the courtesy of Noiseless Typewriters."

Some people won't suffer in silence because that would take the pleasure out of it.

Wisdom is made up of ten parts, nine of which are silence—the tenth, brevity.

He who does not understand your silence will probably not understand your words.

Absolute silence—that's one thing a sportswriter can quote accurately. *Bobby Knight*

Reputation

If you want favor with both God and
man, and a reputation for good
judgment and common sense, then
trust the Lord completely; don't
ever trust yourself.

Proverbs 3:4-5

If you must choose, take a good name
rather than great riches; for to be
held in loving esteem is better
than silver and gold.

Proverbs 22:1

Reputation

Reputation is made in a moment; character is built in a life-time.

Your reputation can be damaged by the opinions of others. Only you yourself can damage character.

Take care of your character, and your reputation will take care of itself.

Few things are more dangerous to a person's reputation than having nothing to do and plenty of time in which to do it.

Reputation is what men say about you on your tombstone; character is what angels say about you before the throne of God. *William Hersey Davis*

Live in such a way that when death comes the mourners will outnumber the cheering section.

Associate yourself with men of good quality if you esteem your own reputation, for it is better to be alone than in bad company. *George Washington*

There are two very difficult things in the world. One is to make a name for oneself and the other is to keep it. *Walter Schumann*

A good reputation is more valuable than the most expensive perfume. *Ecclesiastes 7:1*

Your reputation is made by searching for things that can't be done—and doing them.

Self-Control

Self-control means controlling
the tongue! A quick retort can
ruin everything.
Proverbs 13:3

A wise man controls his temper.
He knows that anger causes mistakes.
Proverbs 14:29

It is better to be slow-tempered than
famous; it is better to have
self-control than to control an army.
Proverbs 16:32

Self-Control

When your output is more than your income, your upkeep may be your downfall.

The man who wants to save face should keep the lower part shut.

Hot words never never resulted in cool judgment.

When upset, count to ten before speaking. When very angry, count to a hundred; then don't speak.

Good advice infrequently taken: No thyself.

The emptier the pot, the quicker the boil—watch your temper.

The man who loses his head is usually the last one to miss it.

In an argument the best weapon to hold is your tongue.

At no time is self-control more difficult than in times of success.

What chance can a man have to control his destiny when he can't control himself?

Self-expression is good; self-control is better.

The best time to keep your shirt on is when you're hot under the collar.

Whether you're on the road or in an argument, when you see red it's time to stop.

Success

The whole city celebrates a good
man's success—and also the
godless man's death.
Proverbs 11:10

———

Plans go wrong with too few
counselors; many counselors
bring success.
Proverbs 15:22

———

Commit your work to the Lord,
then it will succeed.
Proverbs 16:3

Success

Did you hear about the fellow who climbed the ladder of success wrong by wrong?

He who wants to be the top dog must get off the porch.

The secret to success is to do the common things uncommonly well. *John D. Rockefeller Jr.*

A successful man keeps on looking for work after he has found a job.

The Lord has given us two ends,
They have a common link;
For with the bottom end we sit,
And with the other think.
Success in life depends upon
Which end you choose to use,
You'll discover this, my friend,
Heads you win, and tails you lose!

A successful man is one who can lay a firm foundation with the bricks that others throw at him. *David Brinkley*

One of the biggest troubles with success is that its recipe is often the same as that for a nervous breakdown.

This year's success was last year's impossibility.

It's great to be great, but it's greater to be human. *Will Rogers*

When success turns your head, you're facing failure.

Success is a journey, not a destination. *Ben Sweetland*

The secret to success is to be like a duck—smooth and unruffled on top, but paddling furiously underneath.

He who wants milk should not set himself in the middle of the pasture, waiting for a cow to back up to him.

Sometimes it is not good enough to do your best; you have to do what's required. *Sir Winston Churchill*

Success can be measured in dollars and sense.

Becoming number one is easier than remaining number one. *Senator Bill Bradley*

Success is the ability to hitch your wagon to a star while keeping your feet on the ground.

Success is facing up to a no-win situation—and winning anyhow.

I have learned that success is to be measured not so much by the position one has reached in life as by the obstacles he has overcome while trying to succeed. *Booker T. Washington*

Success humbles the great man, astonishes the common man, and puffs up the little man.

Success is sweet, but its secret is sweat.

Success comes in cans; failure comes in can'ts.

Man owes his success to two people: his wife and the Joneses.

Success that goes to your head usually pays a short visit.

Isn't it a shame that when success turns someone's head it doesn't wring his neck at the same time.

Success is relative—the more success, the more relatives.

Success is getting what you want; happiness is wanting what you get.

Even a woodpecker owes his success to the fact that he uses his head.

Successful people are failures who keep getting up, moving on, reaching out, and trying again.

I couldn't wait for success, so I went ahead without it.
Jonathan Winters

The road to success is always under construction.

There are three rules for success. The first: Go on. The second: Go on. And the third: Go on. *Frank Crane*

He who wants to finish the race must stay on the track.

Teaching

A wise teacher makes learning a joy; a
rebellious teacher spouts foolishness.

Proverbs 15:2

Teaching

A schoolteacher is one who must take a lot of live wires and see that they are grounded.

A teacher affects eternity; he can never tell where influence stops. *Henry Adams*

The best teacher follows his own instruction.

Learn of the skillful: He that teaches himself hath a fool for his master. *Benjamin Franklin*

Temptation

How can a young man stay pure? By reading your Word and following its rules. I have tried my best to find you—don't let me wander off from your instructions. I have thought much about your words and stored them in my heart so that they would hold me back from sin.

Psalm 119:9-11

———

Listen to me, young men, and not only listen but obey; don't let your desires get out of hand; don't let yourself think about her. Don't go near her; stay away from where she walks, lest she tempt you and seduce you.

Proverbs 7:24-25

Temptation

He who flees temptation should not leave a forwarding address.

Opportunity knocks only once; temptation leans on the door-bell.

Man's chief merit consists of resisting the impulses of his nature. *Samuel Johnson*

Satan is not such a fool as to fish without bait.

If God bolts the door, do not climb through the window.

No one can be caught in places he does not visit.

You are not tempted because you are evil; you are tempted because you are human.

When you meet temptation, turn to the right.

Opportunity knocks, but temptation kicks the door down.

Unless there is within us that which is above us, we will soon yield to that which is around us.

It is better to shun the bait than to struggle on the hook.

Temptations are like bums—treat one nice, and he will return with many of his friends.

Nothing makes temptation so easy as being broke.

Tenacity

Getting wisdom is the most important
thing you can do!
Proverbs 4:7

———

Steady plodding brings prosperity;
hasty speculation brings poverty.
Proverbs 21:5

———

Don't you know that this good man,
though you trip him up seven times,
will each time rise again?
Proverbs 24:16

Tenacity

Prayer: Lord, give me the tenacity and determination of a weed.

The difference between the impossible and the possible lies in a man's determination. *Tommy Lasorda*

He who wants to move mountains starts by carrying away small stones.

If Christopher Columbus had turned back, no one would have blamed him. No one would have remembered him, either.

He who stands for nothing is apt to fall for anything.

If you don't stand for something, you'll fall for anything.

Only a mediocre person is always at his best.

Mediocrity is a sin. Don't do your bit; do your best. *Admiral "Bull" Halsey*

Today's mighty oak is just yesterday's nut that held its ground.

No person in the world has more determination than he who can stop after eating one peanut.

We stand true to the Lord whether others honor us or despise us, whether they criticize us or commend us. We are honest, but they call us liars. The world ignores us, but we are known to God; we live close to death, but here we are, still very much alive. We have been injured but kept from death. Our hearts ache, but at the same time we have the joy of the Lord. We are poor, but we give rich spiritual gifts to others. We own nothing, and yet we enjoy everything. *2 Corinthians 6:8-10*

You fall the way you lean.

Thankfulness

Gentle words cause life and health;
griping brings discouragement.
Proverbs 15:4

———

If you have good eyesight and good
hearing, thank God who gave
them to you.
Proverbs 20:12

Thankfulness

Gratitude is the heart's memory. *French proverb*

He who forgets the language of gratitude can never be on speaking terms with happiness.

Be thankful for your problems. For if they were less difficult, someone with less ability would have your job.

Look backward with gratitude and forward with confidence.

A war movie being shown on French television showed an American GI pointing to the horizon. "Yanks!" he said to another GI, and the caption read, *"Merci!"*

Disregard your complaints and discover your gratitude. Release your trouble and restate your blessings.

He who receives a good turn should never forget it; he who does one should never remember it.

The worst possible moment for an atheist is when he feels grateful and has no one to thank.

Be grateful for the doors of opportunity—and for friends who oil the hinges.

Happiness comes when we stop wailing about the troubles we have, and offer thanks for all the troubles we don't have.

There's one thing for which you should be deeply grateful: Only you and God have all the facts about you.

Time

Teach us to number our days aright,
that we may gain a heart of wisdom.
Psalm 90:12, NIV

———

To every thing there is a season, and a
time to every purpose under
the heaven.
Ecclesiastes 3:1, KJV

———

It's wonderful to be young! Enjoy
every minute of it! . . . But realize
that you must account to God
for everything you do. . . . Youth,
with a whole life before it, can
make serious mistakes.
Ecclesiastes 11:9-10

Time

If you think time heals everything, try waiting in a doctor's office.

Time is so powerful it is given to us only in small doses.

Sign in New Zealand department store clock display: "There's no present like the time."

Insurance salesman: "Don't you want your office furnishings insured against theft?"
Office manager: "Yes, all except the clock. Everyone watches that!"

Sign over college classroom clock: "Time will pass; will you?"

Time is money. *Benjamin Franklin*

Counting time is not so important as making time count.

I have so much to do today that I shall spend the first three hours in prayer. *Martin Luther*

Those who make the worst use of their time are the first to complain of its shortness. *Jean de la Bruyere*

By the time you get your shoulder to the wheel, your nose to the grindstone, and your ear to the ground, it's usually time for lunch.

Don't let yesterday use up too much of today. *Will Rogers*

Factory sign: "If you have nothing to do, please don't do it here!"

Since time flies, it's up to you to be the navigator.

Some people can stay longer in an hour than others can in a week.

Most of our troubles stem from too much time on our hands and not enough on our knees.

Time is a circus always packing up and moving away.
Ben Hecht

Time goes, you say? Ah, no! Alas, time stays, we go! *Henry David Thoreau*

Satan doesn't care how lofty your intentions may be as long as they are focused on tomorrow.

Time is a great healer, but a poor beautician. *Lucille S. Harper*

Hard work means prosperity; only a fool idles away his time.
Proverbs 12:11

Time and tide wait for no man, but time always stands still for a woman of thirty. *Robert Frost*

The guy who watches the clock will never be the man of the hour.

Sign on office bulletin board: "In case of fire, don't panic. Simply flee the building with the same reckless abandon that occurs each day at quitting time."

I never think of the future. It comes soon enough.

Teacher: "Johnny, name a great time-saver."
Johnny: "Love at first sight."

Time doesn't heal, but it makes the hurt bearable.

Why is it that the fellow who has an hour to kill spends it with someone who doesn't?

Take time to work—it is the price of success
Take time to think—it is the source of power.
Take time to play—it is the secret of youth
Take time to read—it is the foundation of knowledge.
Take time to laugh—it is the music of the soul.
Take time to be courteous—it is the work of a gentleman.
Take time to pray—it is the Christian's vital breath.

Nothing arrives more slowly and passes more quickly than a vacation.

Remember, when you kill time it has no resurrection.

One week, a politician may be on the cover of *Time*; the next, he may be serving it.

One of the worst things about retirement is that you have to drink coffee on your own time.

Tomorrow/Today/Yesterday

Teach us to number our days and
recognize how few they are; help us
to spend them as we should.

Psalm 90:12

———

But the good man walks along in the
ever-brightening light of God's favor;
the dawn gives way to morning
splendor, while the evil man gropes
and stumbles in the dark.

Proverbs 4:18-19

———

Don't brag about your plans for
tomorrow—wait and see
what happens.

Proverbs 27:1

Tomorrow/Today/
Yesterday

Lament: Yesterday was such a bad day; even my twin sister forgot my birthday!

Yesterday's unfinished task is a mortgage on today.

Yesterday's hits won't win today's ball game.

Don't let yesterday use up too much of today. *Will Rogers*

Yesterday is a canceled check; tomorrow is a promissory note; today is the only cash you have—so spend it wisely. *Kay Lyons*

Never put off till tomorrow what you can do the day after tomorrow. *Mark Twain*

Do it tomorrow; you've made enough mistakes for one day. *Bumper sticker*

Today is the tomorrow we worried about yesterday.

Every tomorrow has two handles; we can take hold of the handle of anxiety or the handle of faith. *Henry Ward Beecher*

Procrastination is the art of keeping up to yesterday.

Trouble

Better a little with reverence for God
than great treasure and trouble
with it.
Proverbs 15:16

———

An unreliable messenger can cause
a lot of trouble. Reliable
communication permits progress.
Proverbs 13:17

———

There is treasure in being good, but
trouble dogs the wicked.
Proverbs 15:6

Trouble

A good deal of trouble has been caused in the world by too much intelligence and too little wisdom.

The best way to meet trouble is to face it.

The trouble with the tongue is that it is only three inches long, yet it can kill a man six feet tall.

The only fellow whose troubles are all behind him is a school bus driver.

Never trouble trouble until trouble troubles you.

The best way to ease your own troubles is to help others in theirs.

When you're in deep water, the best thing to do is shut your mouth.

Keep your mouth closed and you'll stay out of trouble.
Proverbs 21:23

It isn't the mountains that trip people up, but the molehills.

Most people have no trouble making ends meet; their feet are always in their mouths.

It's better to sleep on something before doing it, than to do it wrong and stay awake worrying.

The trouble with being a grouch is that you have to make new friends every few months.

Truth

Telling the truth gives a man great
satisfaction, and hard work returns
many blessings to him.
Proverbs 12:14

———

A good man is known by his
truthfulness; a false man by
deceit and lies.
Proverbs 12:17

———

Truth stands the test of time;
lies are soon exposed.
Proverbs 12:19

Truth

The truth will set you free—but first it will make you mad.

Men occasionally stumble over the truth, but most of them pick themselves up and hurry off as if nothing had happened.

Beware of a half-truth; you may get hold of the wrong half.

The greatest homage we can pay to truth is to use it.

Those who stretch the truth usually find that it snaps back.

A diplomatic teacher sent this note home to all parents: "If you promise not to believe everything your child says happens at school, I'll promise not to believe everything he says happens at home."

There are some people so addicted to exaggeration that they can't tell the truth without lying.

A witness who tells the truth saves good men from being sentenced to death, but a false witness is a traitor. *Proverbs 14:25*

Truth is like the sun—all that hides it is a passing cloud.

In quarreling, the truth is always lost.

Anytime you find the truth standing in your way, you may be sure you are heading in the wrong direction.

Father: "I want an explanation and I want the truth."
Son: "Make up your mind, Dad; you can't have both."

Those who never retract their opinions love themselves more than they love truth.

Vision

If you love sleep, you will end in
poverty. Stay awake, work hard, and
there will be plenty to eat!
Proverbs 20:13

———

Where there is no vision,
the people perish.
Proverbs 29:18, KJV

Vision

The degree of vision that dwells in a man is a correct measure of the man. *Carlyle*

Some people who think they are dreamers are just sleepers.

Grass at eye level is taller than the trees half a mile away.

Remember when a fellow with his ear to the ground was a politician? Now he's just a person looking for a lost contact lens.

Wisdom

Every young man who listens to me
and obeys my instructions will be
given wisdom and good sense.

Proverbs 2:1-2

———

The Lord grants wisdom! His every
word is a treasure of knowledge and
understanding. For wisdom and truth
will enter the very center of your
being, filling your life with joy.

Proverbs 2:6, 10

Wisdom

Wise men change their minds; fools never.

No man really becomes a fool until he stops asking questions. *Charles P. Steinmetz*

He who asks a question may be a fool for five minutes; he who never asks a question remains a fool forever.

The door of wisdom swings on hinges of common sense and uncommon thoughts. *William Arthur Ward*

Thinking well is wise; planning well is wiser; doing well is wisest of all.

The doorstep to the temple of wisdom is a knowledge of our own ignorance. *Charles Spurgeon*

Some are wise, and some are otherwise.

Everybody is ignorant, only on different subjects. *Will Rogers*

He who thinks education is costly ought to try ignorance.

There is nothing more frightful than ignorance in action. *Goethe*

Stupidity is forever; ignorance can be fixed.

If fifty million people say a foolish thing, it is still a foolish thing. *Anatole France*

Intelligence: Spotting a flaw in the boss's character. Wisdom: Not mentioning it.

If ignorance is bliss, why aren't more people happy?

I don't think much of a man who is not wiser today than he was yesterday. *Abraham Lincoln*

A fool is his own informer. *Yiddish proverb*

If wisdom's way you'd wisely seek,
Five things observe with care;
Of whom you speak, to whom you speak,
And how and why and where.

Knowledge is horizontal; wisdom is vertical and comes from above. *Billy Graham*

Wisdom is knowing what to do next, skill is knowing how to do it, and virtue is doing it. *David S. Jordan*

Nine-tenths of wisdom is being wise on time.
Theodore Roosevelt

He who is wise by day is no fool by night.

The wise are promoted to honor, but fools are promoted to shame! *Proverbs 3:35*

When you have got an elephant by the hind legs and he is trying to run away, it's best to let him run. *Abraham Lincoln*

A wise man thinks all he says; a fool says all he thinks.

A wise husband will buy his wife such fine china that she won't trust him to wash the dishes.

I would rather be the man who bought the Brooklyn Bridge than the one who sold it. *Will Rogers*

A wise person has an open mind and a closed mouth.

A wise man is like a tack—sharp and pointed in the right direction.

God, grant me the serenity to accept the things I cannot change; the courage to change the things I can; and the wisdom to know the difference. *Reinhold Niebuhr*

The wisest man remembers that to catch a mouse you starve a cat.

As a person grows wiser, he talks less and says more.

A wise man will never plant more garden than his wife can hoe.

Wisdom enables one to be thrifty without being stingy, and generous without being wasteful.

Woman/Wife

Honor goes to kind and gracious
women, mere money to cruel men.

Proverbs 11:16

———

A worthy wife is her husband's joy
and crown; the other kind corrodes
his strength and tears down
everything he does.

Proverbs 12:4

Woman / Wife

A word to the wife is sufficient, provided that word is yes.

The man of the hour is the one whose wife asked him to wait a minute.

If you don't think women are explosive, try dropping one.

The best time to mow the grass is just after your wife suggests it.

The wife who listens to every word her husband says is probably looking for a hole in his alibi.

Words are powerful. For instance, if you say to a woman, "How cool you look," she's pleased. But try telling her she doesn't look so hot.

It's too bad all women don't marry archaeologists, for the older she gets the more interested he is in her.

A hundred men may make an encampment, but it takes a woman to make a home. *Chinese proverb*

The weaker sex is the stronger sex because of the weakness of the stronger sex for the weaker sex.

When a man answers the phone he reaches for a pencil. A woman grabs a chair.

Certainly, God created man before woman. But then you always make a rough draft before the final masterpiece.

God made woman when man was in his first sleep, and man hasn't had any repose since.

Women can never be as successful as men; they have no wives to advise them.

Most women's magazines have fifty pages of recipes and fifty pages of diets.

Woman has been placed at a disadvantage; man can now travel faster than sound.

After winning an argument with his wife, the wisest thing a man can do is apologize.

The best way to remember your wife's birthday is to forget it once.

The best way to compliment your wife is frequently.

A diplomat is a man who can make his wife believe she would look fat in a fur coat.

The safest way to disagree with your wife is very quietly.

When a man brings his wife flowers for no reason—he'd better have one.

Genuine happiness is when a wife sees a double chin on her husband's old girlfriend.

Many husbands go broke on the money their wives save at sales.

The trouble with wives is that they'd rather mend your ways than your socks.

The best thing about women is that there are so many of them.

Words

Some people like to make cutting
remarks, but the words of the
wise soothe and heal.

Proverbs 12:18

———

A gentle answer turns away wrath, but
harsh words cause quarrels.

Proverbs 15:1

———

The Lord hates the thoughts of the
wicked but delights in kind words.

Proverbs 15:26

Words

Water and words—easy to pour, impossible to recover.

The person of few words doesn't have to recall so many.

You can never speak a kind word too soon, for you never know how soon it will be too late.

The spoken word is like an arrow. You cannot call it back.

If you would be pungent, be brief, for it is with words as with sunbeams; the more they are condensed, the deeper they burn. *Robert Southey*

A second wind is what some preachers get when they say, "And now in conclusion."

The difference between the right word and the almost right word is the difference between lightning and the lightning bug. *Mark Twain*

He who speaks much is much mistaken.

If all who speak would weigh their words, how light the air would be!

He who says nothing shows a fine command of language.

Work

Work brings profit; talk brings
poverty!
Proverbs 14:23

———

If you won't plow in the cold, you
won't eat at the harvest.
Proverbs 20:4

———

Do you know a hard-working man?
He shall be successful and
stand before kings!
Proverbs 22:29

Work

Providence sends food for the birds but does not throw it in the nest.

One thing you can learn by watching the clock is that it passes the time by keeping its hands busy.

The more steam you put into your work, the louder you can whistle when the work is done.

It is better for you to wear out than to rust out.

He who rolls up sleeves seldom loses shirt.

Most of the world's useful work is done by people who are pressed for time, or are tired, or don't feel well.

The only place where success comes before work is in the dictionary.

I like work; it fascinates me. I can sit and watch it for hours. I love to keep it by me; the idea of getting rid of it nearly breaks my heart. *Jerome*

Hard work brings prosperity; playing around brings poverty. *Proverbs 28:19*

I never did anything worth doing by accident, nor did any of my inventions come by accident; they came by work. *Thomas Edison*

The best way to hear money jingle in your pocket is to shake a leg.

You can never make your dreams come true by oversleeping.

If you want to work *for* God, form a committee. If you want to work *with* God, form a prayer group.

Most people work for a good cause: 'cause they need the money.

The only workout some folks get is jumping to conclusions, running down their friends, sidestepping their responsibility, and pushing their luck.

Poverty passes by a hardworking man's door.

Don't knock the Puritan ethic: hard work for hard work's sake. With it, they built a new nation without taking a coffee break!

Workers of the world, unite! You have nothing to lose but your receivables!

Actually, most people aren't afraid of hard work. They fight it year after year.

The second-laziest worker on earth is the one who joined as many unions as he could to make sure he was always on strike.

Work for the Lord. The pay isn't much, but the retirement plan is out of this world.

Soap, water, and elbow grease; those are the three ingredients for success in the hotel business. *Conrad Hilton*

The difference between an amateur and a professional is this: An amateur hopes; a professional works.
Oscar Hammerstein II

A turning wheel does not get rusty.

Nothing is work unless you would rather be doing something else.

There are many essential oils in industry, but the best one is still elbow grease.

Even a mosquito doesn't get a slap on the back until he starts to work.

The worst day of fishing beats the best day at work.
Bumper sticker

Housework never killed anyone—but why take chances?

I owe, I owe, it's off to work I go.

The world is full of willing people; some willing to work, the rest willing to let them. *Robert Frost*

My boss advised me to work eight hours and sleep eight hours—only it shouldn't be the same hours!

We specialize in patios, terraces, and necking. Phone Clive after hours. *Classified ad under Work Wanted*

He who wishes to eat in the evening must be willing to work during the day.

He who cuts his own wood warms himself twice.

He who wants to leave footprints in the sands of time must wear work boots.

Zeal

Yes, if you want better insight and discernment, and are searching for them as you would for lost money or hidden treasure, then wisdom will be given you and knowledge of God himself; you will soon learn the importance of reverence for the Lord and of trusting him.

Proverbs 2:3-5

———

You will find me when you seek me, if you look for me in earnest.

Jeremiah 29:13

Z e a l

No one gives his opinion with more zeal than an ignorant person.

Enthusiasm is the best protection in any situation.

What the world needs is more young people who will carry to their jobs the same enthusiasm for getting ahead that they display in traffic.

The best way to get rid of your duties is to zealously discharge them.

Duty without enthusiasm becomes laborious; duty with enthusiasm becomes glorious. *William Arthur Ward*

The person who has no fire in himself cannot ignite others.

Be zealous for God; remember, more people chase fire engines than ice wagons!

A wise man once said that enthusiasm is nothing but faith with a tin can tied to its tail.

If it were as easy to arouse enthusiasm as it is to arouse suspicion, just think what could be accomplished!

Enthusiasm extinguishes the gloom in the room. *Frank Tyger*